D0454106

THE
CURÉ OF ARS

THE
CURÉ OF ARS

THE STORY OF SAINT JOHN VIANNEY
PATRON SAINT OF PARISH PRIESTS

By
Mary Fabyan Windeatt

Illustrated by
Gedge Harmon

TAN BOOKS AND PUBLISHERS, INC.
Rockford, Illinois 61105

Nihil Obstat: Fintan Walker, Ph.D.
                  Francis Reine, S.T.D.
                  Censores Librorum

Imprimatur: ✠ Paul C. Schulte, D.D.
                  Archbishop of Indianapolis
                  May 17, 1947
                  Feast of St. Paschal Baylon

Copyright © 1947 by St. Meinrad's Abbey Inc., St. Meinrad, Indiana.

This work first appeared in serial form in the pages of *The Catholic Home Messenger*. As a book, it was originally published under the title *The Parish Priest of Ars: The Story of Saint John Marie Vianney*.

Retypeset by TAN Books and Publishers, Inc. The type in this book is the property of TAN Books and Publishers, Inc., and may not be reproduced, in whole or in part, without written permission from the Publisher. (This restriction applies only to reproduction of *this type*, not to quotations from the book.)

ISBN: 0-89555-418-6

Library of Congress Catalog Card No.: 90-71827

Printed and bound in the United States of America.

TAN BOOKS AND PUBLISHERS, INC.
P.O. Box 424
Rockford, Illinois 61105

1991

To every boy
who wants to be
a priest—
and to every priest
who wants to be
another Curé of Ars.

CONTENTS

THE
CURÉ OF ARS

CHAPTER ONE

Shepherd Boy

M Y NAME is John, and I have been dead since August 4, 1859. How happy I am! For my soul is in Heaven. Yes, for eternity I am privileged to see God. . .For endless eternity I enjoy a happiness that is beyond the power of mere words to describe. And nothing can ever take this happiness from me! Or from my friends—the millions of men and women and boys and girls who are with me in Paradise! For the joy we have is everlasting. It is eternal. God has said so, and of course He cannot lie.

It was not easy to win this joy. When a soul comes into the world, the Devil tries very hard to drag it down to Hell. So it was with nearly everyone who is in Heaven today, the chief exceptions being those who died shortly after Baptism—babies and very small children. But I—well, my life on earth lasted

1

for more than seventy-three years, and many, many times during that period the Devil tried to discourage me in my efforts to please God and to win the place which He had prepared for me in Paradise.

Did he succeed? Of course not. And why? Because of the wonderful courage God gave me whenever I called upon Him. For in my day (even as in any day) whenever there was a temptation to do wrong, to go over to the Devil's side and give up the struggle to win Heaven, God was always ready with His grace. Since He wills that every soul in the world shall someday enjoy the good things of Heaven, naturally He does not withhold the means to obtain them. But what a pity that so few people understand this, and that when trials and temptations come they never think of asking God for the grace to remain true to Him. Because of such neglect, the struggle against the Devil is generally far harder than it needs to be. Many times, alas, it even ends in defeat—in Hell, with all its terrible darkness and misery and pain.

My struggle to outwit the Devil and to win Heaven (although it was some time before I really understood about such things) began on May 8, 1786, in Dardilly, a village not far from the city of Lyons, in France. My parents, Matthew Vianney and Maria Beluse, already had three children: Catherine, Jane and Francis. But they were delighted to have still another, and on the same day that I was born I was taken to the village church to be baptized. Here I was given two names: John, in honor of Saint John the Baptist, and Marie (the French form of Mary) in honor of the Blessed Virgin.

"I wonder what little John Marie Vianney will be when he grows up?" some of the neighbors asked one another thoughtfully. "He seems to be a fine, strong boy."

"Why, he'll be a farmer like his father," was the general opinion.

The reply was certainly a natural one. For generations my people had tilled the soil. What was more likely than that I should follow in their footsteps? And follow in their footsteps I did, at least during the early years of my life. Of course my tasks were just simple ones at first, such as feeding the chickens, gathering the eggs, weeding the garden. But when I was seven years old my father made an important announcement.

"John, I think you're big enough now for real work," he said. "Tomorrow you may take the sheep to pasture."

How happy I was at this new responsibility! My brother Francis, two years older than I, had been in charge of the flocks for some time. Now I was considered trustworthy enough to take his place. Now I would be allowed to be away from home all day, seeing that the sheep found good grazing land, that they did not eat weeds which would make them sick, that they did not stray into neighbors' fields, that they came to no harm from other animals. And if I did my work well, nine-year-old Francis could be spared for still other duties on the farm.

So it was that I became a shepherd. Frequently my little sister Marguerite (who was seventeen months younger than I and whose pet name was Gothon) accompanied me into the fields. Then, when the sheep were peacefully grazing, we played games with neighboring shepherd children who came to visit us. However, there were many days when the other children did not come. At such times Gothon and I played by ourselves or knitted stockings.

Perhaps to children in America it may seem strange that a boy should know how to knit. In my day this was not considered strange at all. Every country child was expected to make himself useful, even when he was quite small. And since we were very hard on our stockings, our mother taught us how to make new ones with the wool from our own sheep.

I had been born in 1786. Shortly afterwards, many political disturbances arose throughout France. In the year when I was given charge of my father's flocks, godless men had long been in control of the government. Churches and monasteries were closed. All priests and nuns who acknowledged the Pope as Head of the Church were hunted down as though they were wild beasts, and cruelly murdered. Finally, unless one were willing to pay with his life, it was no longer possible to attend the Holy Sacrifice of the Mass or to receive the Sacraments.

"Children, our country is being punished for its sins," said my mother sorrowfully. "Oh, what a dreadful thing it is to offend the good God! See what hardship and pain it brings, even to the innocent!"

I was just a seven-year-old boy, but my mother's words made a deep impression on me. And I was even more grieved when I heard that there were priests who, to protect themselves, had sworn to uphold the new government. These continued to say Mass publicly, although of course no good Catholic would attend.

"There are many brave priests, though, who refuse to have anything to do with the wicked government," my mother told us. "They are in hiding."

"In hiding?" I asked curiously, not quite understanding what this phrase meant.

"Yes. They dress like farmers or peddlers or tramps. But they are priests just the same. Perhaps it will be possible for us to go to their Masses."

For several years we managed to do just that. Late at night (as though we were bent on committing some great crime) we would creep from our beds and walk the mile or more to the barn or farmhouse which had been selected as a meeting place. All of us children were sworn to the utmost secrecy, and never would we have dreamed of mentioning to any stranger what we were doing or where we were going at that hour of the night without so much as a candle or a lantern to guide us over the rough country road. We would rather have died than betray the whereabouts of a priest who had remained faithful to the Pope, and who that very night would hear Confessions, offer Mass and give Holy Communion to his little flock.

Of course I was all eyes and ears when we finally reached the makeshift church—especially for the priest, who was risking death to bring us farmer folk the consolations of our Holy Faith. What a brave man he was! How wise! How holy! And yet in appearance he was just like anyone else. . .

"But he isn't just like anyone else," my mother whispered. "Even in Heaven he will be set apart from other men."

And then as best she could, she explained about the priesthood—how it is a supernatural state of life to which God calls certain men, so that they may become channels for His grace. Through these men, who take the place of Christ on earth, God pours forth His love and mercy. Through them He receives the greatest prayer the world can ever know—the Sacrifice of the Mass. Through them He takes away the stain of Original Sin in Baptism, in Confession forgives any sin it is possible for man to commit, in the Holy Eucharist gives Himself as food to struggling mankind, and in Confirmation sends the Holy Spirit to help souls profess and spread the Catholic Faith. Through priests He unites men and women in the holy partnership of marriage, prepares the souls of the dying to enter into eternity, and in Holy Orders gives the same powers to other men, so that the priesthood will last as long as the world itself.

I often thought about my mother's words. How wonderful to be chosen by God to be a priest! How fortunate were those boys who, having received the call, had the chance to study the many things necessary to fulfill this vocation! So carried away was I by such thoughts that before long an idea for a fine new game had presented itself. I, seven-year-old John Marie Vianney, would make believe that God was

WE PRETENDED THAT I WAS A PRIEST

calling me to be a priest. Even more. I would not be simply a student. I would be already ordained. I would have the right to preach and to conduct church services.

With a little coaxing, Gothon and the other shepherd children joined in the new pastime and agreed to be my congregation. Thus, each day while the sheep were peacefully grazing, we said the Rosary, sang hymns and marched in procession through the fields behind a makeshift cross. Later I preached a sermon—but only a short one, because my listeners were not partial to long speeches. Occasionally we also gathered before a little clay statue of the Blessed Virgin which I had made (I kept it hidden in a tree trunk near the brook) and decorated it with moss and wildflowers.

So the years passed—1793, 1794, 1795. Religious persecution still went on in France, and although certain loyal Catholic families managed to attend Mass, they still had to do so in secret. As a result, it was impossible for us younger country children to make our First Confessions, or to receive Holy Communion, since there was no way for us to have regular instructions from the various priests who moved from one village to another under constant threat of death. Indeed, I was eleven years old before I went to Confession, and thirteen years old before I received my First Communion.

Probably this great event would have been postponed even longer had I not been able to spend some months visiting Aunt Marguerite, my mother's sister, in the neighboring town of Ecully. Here lived several priests (although a stranger would have taken one for a cook, another for a shoemaker, a third for a carpenter, so successfully had these servants of God disguised themselves in order to escape capture by the police). There were also two good women in Ecully who had been nuns in the Congregation of Saint Charles before the government had driven them into exile.

"My nephew John Marie has never been to school," Aunt Marguerite told these faithful souls. "Do you suppose you could teach him a little reading and writing? And something about the Catechism?"

Father Groboz (who worked as a cook) and Father Balley (who worked as a carpenter) agreed to do what they could for me. So did the two women who had been nuns.

"John Marie may join the First Communion class," they said. "There are fifteen other children already enrolled."

The time and place for the meetings of the First Communion class were as secret as those for the Holy Sacrifice, and the danger was as great for both teachers and pupils. For instance, what would happen if the police came when we were studying our Catechism? How could we explain why we were gathered there? Suppose we became excited and let slip some information about the priests and nuns who were our teachers? Yet the weeks passed, no police came, and finally the beautiful day of First Communion arrived.

How happy I was to receive Our Lord! What did

it matter that there were no white dresses for the girls, no new suits for the boys? That the great event was not taking place in a flower-decked church but in a farmhouse with wagonloads of hay drawn up before the windows so that no godless stranger could tell what was going on inside? I did not think of any of these things. All that mattered was that at last Our Lord had come—He, who could make my soul clean and pleasing to Him. . .Who could help me to do my work well. . .

"I love You, dear Lord," I said. "But I know that I can love You still more if only You will show me how. Will You? Please?"

CHAPTER TWO

The Struggle Begins

NOW that I had had some schooling and had made my First Communion, my parents decided that I had stayed long enough with Aunt Marguerite and should return to Dardilly.

"You're a big boy, John," my father told me. "It's time that you helped with the heavy work at home."

So eleven-year-old Gothon and nine-year-old Francis were given charge of the sheep, while I began to help my fifteen-year-old brother (whose name was also Francis) with a variety of tasks. Some days we plowed the barley field or worked around the grape-vines. On others, we dug trenches, pruned the trees, gathered wood, pitched hay, cared for the cattle, picked fruit, searched for nuts or tended the wine-press. Truly, there were no idle moments for either of us boys, and at first I was inclined to be just a little discouraged.

"No matter how hard I try, I can't work as fast as you do," I told my brother one day. "And I get so tired!"

Francis laughed. "Who expects anything else? Why, I'm nearly two years older than you, and bigger and stronger. It's only natural that I should be able to do more."

"Yes. But it would be nice if I could keep up just a little better. . ."

The weeks passed, and Francis continued to do far more work than I. Then suddenly I hit upon a plan. I would ask the Blessed Virgin for help! Each morning I would take a small statue of her with me when we went into the fields, hide it in a place well in advance of where we were working, then make a real effort to reach the statue quickly.

"Dear Blessed Mother, please let this plan work!" I begged earnestly.

From the start the new plan did work, and so well that soon it was Francis' turn to be tired and discouraged. One day when we had been weeding the fields, he looked at me with real admiration.

"You're doing far more work than you used to," he remarked. "What's happened, John? What's your secret?"

At first I wasn't too anxious to explain how each morning I said a special prayer to the Blessed Virgin Mother, kissed the feet of her little statue and threw it as far as I could into the field, took up my hoe and began to cut down weeds as though my life depended on it, then repeated the entire procedure when I had reached the statue. But finally

I told my story. The Blessed Mother was helping me. It was far easier to work, even at such a lowly task as weeding, when she was the inspiration and the goal.

For a moment Francis was silent. Then his eyes brightened. "I guess you're right," he said slowly. "From now on I'll ask the Blessed Mother to help me, too."

Eventually the persecution which had closed French churches and monasteries for so many years came to an end. In the spring of 1802, when I was sixteen years old, Catholics throughout the country once more were able to profess their faith without fear. Priests and nuns returned to their former posts. Church bells, large and small, pealed out joyfully as once again the Holy Sacrifice was offered with fitting pomp and splendor.

How thrilled I was at this! And how delighted that in nearby Ecully, Father Balley had announced that he was looking for boys who wanted to study for the priesthood! So many faithful pastors had been murdered during the Revolution that now there was a great shortage of priests. Until the crisis was over, he would take any deserving student into his rectory and personally supervise the first part of his long and difficult training.

"Perhaps he'd take me," I thought hopefully. "Oh, how wonderful that would be!"

Yes, since those childhood days when I had conducted make-believe church services for Gothon and our little shepherd friends in the fields, I had dreamed longingly of the priesthood. What a glorious state of life it was! Through the priesthood one human being might awaken countless other human beings to a knowledge and love of God. And not just an ordinary knowledge and love. Ah, no! A worthy priest could do far more than this. Because he is privileged to offer to the Heavenly Father the Body and Blood of His Son in the Holy Sacrifice, he has a constant and special access to all the graces which the Heavenly Father has in store for mankind. To put it plainly (as my mother had done so often on those midnight journeys to the secret Masses) a priest is a channel for God's love and mercy. He is another Christ, and if he so wills to use fully the wonderful powers given to him, he can work miracles in human hearts. Of lukewarm souls, and even of sinners, he can make saints.

But I, sixteen-year-old John Marie Vianney, knew so little! Why, I could barely read and write! How could I ever hope to learn Latin and philosophy and theology and all the other subjects required of a candidate for the priesthood? Then there was Father. On the few occasions when I had dared to speak to him of my secret hope, he had gruffly refused to have anything to do with it. I was a farm boy, he said, with my duties clearly marked out for me at home.

"I should think you'd understand that and not bother me with foolish notions," he declared reproachfully. "Why, with your sister Catherine getting married and needing a dowry, and your big brother Francis arranging to buy a release from the Army, you ought to realize that soon I'll have very little money left...and certainly none to waste on sending a big boy like you to school."

I tried not to be hurt at my father's words. He was a fine Christian man, always ready to give food, clothes and lodging to needy strangers who stopped at our farm. But he really believed—and who could blame him?—that for me the priesthood was an impossible goal. After all, I was not like other candidates for the Seminary. My only schooling was that obtained during the few months I had spent visiting Aunt Marguerite in Ecully in preparation for my First Communion. And that was so long ago now—three years!

But I persisted with my argument, at least for a little while. "Father, it wouldn't cost much to *start* my studies," I urged respectfully. "I could live with Aunt Marguerite again, and pay for my room and board by working around the place. As for Father Balley, I don't think he intends to charge his students anything. You see, he's so anxious that our country should have many priests..."

A hard light entered Father's eyes. "Silence!" he said sternly. "I've said that I won't allow you to go to Ecully, and I mean it, John. So don't let me hear about it again."

In the face of such an order, what could I do? Father really believed that I ought to stay at home. By now I was experienced with the farm work. My presence saved him the expense of hiring a helper. And he and Mother were growing old. Surely it was my duty to be with them in their last years?

But Mother did not agree. Her heart flooded with

joy at the thought that God might be calling a son
of hers to the priesthood. Nothing must stand in
the way of such a wonderful grace. All obstacles,
no matter how great, must be overcome.

"We'll pray," she told me confidently. "We'll ask
the good God to change your father's heart. Oh,
John! The Devil always tries very hard to keep a
boy from reaching God's altar, but something tells
me that for you he's going to make things especially
difficult."

Mother was right. One year passed, then two years,
and life on the farm became increasingly difficult
for me. Loving Father as I did, I could understand
his viewpoint—the desire to have me at home, the
reluctance to spend hard-earned money foolishly, the
justifiable fear that I was not clever enough at books
to be able to pass the examinations for the priesthood. Yet oh, how hard it was for me to spend each
day hoeing in the fields or tending the cattle when
I was longing with my whole heart to be absorbed
in other duties—in studying and praying and learning those things which would help me to become
a priest! Truly, as the months slipped by, I was often
thoroughly discouraged.

"Father will never change his mind," I told myself
sadly. "I just know it. Oh, dear God, what am I
going to do?"

But Mother had real faith. "John, remember what
I told you about the Devil," she often said. "He likes
nothing better than to have young people fall into
sin and so offend the good God. But when he fails
in this, he does his best to make them down-hearted

"WE'LL PRAY," MOTHER SAID CONFIDENTLY.

about one thing or another. In this way, he soon
has them murmuring against God's Will. You don't
want to do that, do you?"

I shook my head. "No, of course not, Mother."

"All right, then. Let's say the Rosary and ask the
Blessed Virgin once more to help you to become
a good and holy priest."

Suddenly, at the end of another difficult year of
waiting, the miracle happened. Father announced
that he would no longer stand in my way if I wished
to study for the priesthood. I might go to Ecully,
and with his blessing.

"You're a good boy," he told me. "And I guess
that what you want to do with your life is more your
affair than mine. Forgive me, my son, if I've been
harsh."

At these words my heart all but burst with happiness. I, now nineteen years of age, might study for
the priesthood after all? Oh, how good God was to
give me a grace that is denied even to the angels!

"Father, I just don't know how to thank you!" I
cried. "I just don't!"

For a long moment Father gazed upon me, a
strange look in his eyes. Then he turned away
abruptly. "Don't thank me," he muttered. "Thank
your mother."

Yet even as I rejoiced, a new obstacle presented
itself to discourage me. Father had indeed given his
permission for me to go to Ecully, but the Devil
was not to be outdone in his efforts to keep me
from the priesthood. A few days later Mother went
eagerly to make arrangements for my entrance into

Father Balley's classes. But she returned home more tired and discouraged than I had ever seen her. The good pastor of Ecully had said that he did not think I had a vocation to the priesthood and had refused to accept me as a student.

I could hardly believe my ears. "Why, Father Balley scarcely knows me!" I burst out. "He...he just remembers me from those few months I spent in Ecully preparing for my First Communion. And I was only thirteen then, and so ignorant! Oh, Mother! Didn't you tell him that I've been studying by myself ever since? That I've read most of the Imitation and a lot from the Gospels and the Lives of the Saints?"

"Yes, I told him, John," said Mother through her tears.

"And he didn't believe you?"

"Of course he believed me. But...well, I guess he thinks that that's not enough. Besides, he explained that his students are far younger than you—boys twelve and fourteen years of age. He said that you'd feel very much out of place among them."

My heart sank even lower when I reflected upon the fact that the parish priest of Ecully, in whom I had placed such trust, was a learned and holy man. If he really believed that I was too old and too stupid to learn anything...if he really didn't want to be bothered with me...

But my discouragement did not last long, for before we went to bed that night Mother's usual cheerfulness had returned. "I'll go to see Father Balley again," she declared firmly. "And you and I

will pray as we've never prayed before. Oh, John!
The Devil must never be allowed to win over us!
Never, never, never!"

CHAPTER THREE

The Struggle Continues

IN THE end it was my sister Catherine's husband who prevailed upon Father Balley to let me come to Ecully for a personal interview. Mother accompanied me on the trip, speaking words of comfort and encouragement all the way.

"You mustn't be afraid, John," she told me. "Father Balley is really a kind man. And his sister is kind, too. She lives at the rectory with him. I know she'll be glad to see you."

Alas! My courage was all but gone when we finally reached Ecully, and I feared I would never be able to utter one sensible word in Father Balley's presence. After all, he was such a clever man, one whom the Major Seminary in Lyons would have been glad to number among its professors. And I? Why, I was just a farm boy—shy, awkward, uneducated.

Yet in the end things turned out splendidly.

Although Father Balley's appearance was somewhat forbidding (he was a thin, serious man who seemed far older than his fifty-two years), there was also something about him that set my heart at ease. Before long I was talking with him quite freely about my longing to become a priest. I was even discussing the few books I had read—the Gospels and the Imitation of Christ—without the least trace of embarrassment.

"Well, John, I guess that you may come here after all," he told me finally. And before I knew it, Mother and he were making arrangements for my entrance into his little school.

Of course there were no words to express my delight. How good God was to have heard my prayers! And the Blessed Virgin! Yet in a few days I realized a disturbing fact: namely (as is so often the case in this world) that I had just exchanged one set of fears and troubles for another. True, Father Balley had accepted me as a student, and thus I was now on the beginning of the long road to the priesthood. But how hard the studies were, Latin in particular! Try though I would, I could make such little progress...

"That's because you're not used to studying," Father Balley said kindly. "You're more accustomed to having a shovel in your hands than a book. But it will get easier after awhile. Wait and see."

Alas! Things did not get easier at all, and after a few weeks it was common knowledge among the other students that the lowest place in each class belonged to me. What matter that I was almost twenty and that they were much younger? My advantage in years only made me seem more stupid.

"John, maybe I could help you with your work," twelve-year-old Matthias Loras suggested one day. "Latin isn't hard, and neither is anything else, if you get things right in the beginning."

I was truly grateful to Matthias. He was a clever youngster, and although neither of us knew it then, God had planned that someday he should go to the United States as a missionary priest and later become the Bishop of Dubuque.

"If you'll help me, I'll pray for you every day," I said. "Truly I will."

So Matthias began to coach me in Latin, going slowly and carefully over each day's lesson. But even he was amazed at my thick-headedness. Then one day he completely lost his patience and boxed my ears.

"You big dumbbell!" he cried angrily. "How many times do I have to tell you a thing before it stays in your head?"

At this all the other boys roared with delight, so that I was thoroughly confused and ashamed. Scarcely knowing what I did, I got to my knees and awkwardly stammered out that I was sorry. Yes, I was a dumbbell. It was a waste of time for Matthias to bother with me.

But a wave of remorse was sweeping through my young instructor. "No, it's not," he said earnestly, and, kneeling also, he put his arms about me. "We'll try again, John. And forgive me for hitting you. I've a wretched temper that's always getting the better of me."

So once again the future Bishop of Dubuque began the lesson, and once again I did my best to understand. But in a few weeks I confided to Father Balley that I felt sure the priesthood was not for me. Only through pride could I have undertaken such an impossible venture.

"I know how to be a farmer and that's all," I muttered. "Will you please give me permission to go home, Father?"

For a long moment the good pastor was silent, his eyes full upon my woebegone face. Then he spoke:

"So this is the end, John? You really don't want to work for souls?"

A pang shot through my heart. *To work for souls!* Oh, how much I wanted to do just that—and as a priest. But how could I when I was so stupid?

"Maybe I could go home just for a visit," I faltered. "Perhaps I could study a bit by myself..."

Quickly Father Balley shook his head. "If your father were to see you now, so discouraged and downhearted, he'd never let you come back. You know that."

"But what shall I do, Father? I can't seem to get anywhere with my studies, no matter how hard I try."

"What about prayer, my son? Have you asked the saints in Heaven to help you?"

"Yes, Father. And especially the Holy Spirit."

"And you've added suffering to your prayer? Little mortifications of one sort or another?"

I nodded. Long ago I had learned the worth of suffering joined to prayer, and ever since I had been staying in Ecully I had tried to make sacrifices in the matter of food and drink. Yet of late an idea for a new kind of sacrifice had presented itself. Suppose I were to go on a pilgrimage somewhere, depending solely on the charity of others for food and lodging. . .

Hesitantly I outlined my plan to Father Balley. If he would not give permission for me to go home, perhaps he would allow me to visit some holy place?

"And where would you like to go, John?"

"To La Louvesc, to the shrine of Saint John Francis Regis," I replied, new hope rising in my heart even as I spoke. "Oh, Father! Perhaps the saints would help me to gain the graces that I need!"

In the end Father Balley blessed the suggestion, and within a few weeks (it was the summer vacation of the year 1806) I set out on my pilgrimage. But very soon I experienced all manner of unexpected difficulties. La Louvesc was in the mountains, some sixty-odd miles from Ecully, and the roads were very poor. To make matters worse, no one believed that I was a student for the priesthood, and whenever I asked for an alms I was rudely refused.

"You're just a tramp," one farmer told me harshly. "Be off with you!"

"A pilgrim to La Louvesc!" sneered another. "Young man, if you don't get going at once, I'll set my dogs on you. I've suffered before from good-for-nothings like you."

"If I let you spend the night here, you'd steal everything I have," declared a third. "I know your kind."

It was all very discouraging, and after two days and nights of steady walking I became very faint. Yet I pushed on somehow—finding shelter at night in the roadside hedges and satisfying my hunger in part with wild herbs and berries.

"Dear Lord, won't You let this suffering win for me the graces that I need?" I begged wearily.

After a little while I met a few kind people who gave me some bread, thus enabling me to journey on with new strength. However, upon reaching La Louvesc and going to Confession, I received some unexpected advice. "Young man, on your return trip you'd better give alms instead of asking for them," the priest told me. "In my opinion, you undertook too much hardship in coming all the way here as a beggar."

Naturally I was taken aback at such advice, for I knew that prayer joined to suffering has a truly extraordinary power to touch the Heart of God. I had learned this from my mother, from the heroic priests who had ministered to us during the dark days of the Revolution, and more recently from my beloved friend and teacher, Father Balley. That was why, with my vocation in peril, I had determined to take upon myself some suffering so that my prayers for help would merit an answer. Now, to be advised to set aside the sacrifice. . .

As respectfully as I could, I explained the things to my confessor. The trip from Ecully had indeed been hard. But surely no price was too high to pay for the grace of perseverance in my studies? And surely it would not be right to break the promise

I FOUND SHELTER IN THE ROADSIDE HEDGES.

which I had made so recently and return home in the manner of other pilgrims—stopping overnight at wayside inns and eating regularly?

For a moment my confessor was silent. Then he spoke: "Sometimes there is great merit in making things easy for ourselves when we had thought to make them hard."

I was really amazed. "There is, Father?"

"Oh, yes. You see, it proves how really weak we are. We thought that we were strong enough to do such and such, and now we discover that it isn't so at all. Oh, my son, if people could just realize one thing!"

"What, Father."

"That sometimes an act of mortification can be tinged with pride, but never an act of obedience."

These words rang in my ears with such insistence that before I left the confessional I had accepted the grace which they implied: namely, to do another's will instead of my own. Yes, I promised the priest (who was truly concerned over my health) that I would return home in the manner of other pilgrims, paying for my meals and lodging and giving alms to any poor person I met. I would no longer run the risk of being rash or imprudent in the matter of mortification.

The priest was pleased at my decision. "I'm sure, because of your obedience, that Saint John Francis Regis will grant the favor you came to ask of him," he said. "And I'm also sure that you'll find much happiness during your stay here."

It was true. The days I passed at La Louvesc were

happy ones. I felt free, at peace with myself and the world. Oh, surely I would be given the grace to learn sufficient Latin so that I might continue with my studies for the priesthood?

Upon returning to Ecully, I found that my prayers had been heard—at least in part. Somehow the dreaded Latin was not quite so difficult as before. I could remember the meanings of new words with less trouble. It was also easier to translate the various passages given to me by Father Balley. Yet I was far from being an expert, and occasionally I became miserably down-hearted. Someday, if I was ever to be ordained, I would have to leave Ecully and enter the Minor Seminary at Verrières. Here I would be required to speak in Latin from time to time, and even to follow entire lectures in it. Oh, how could I ever accomplish such difficult things?

"We won't worry about that just now," Father Balley said comfortingly. "The main thing is, your trip to La Louvesc was a success, John. You're improving in your studies—very slowly, of course, but surely."

I continued to make still more slow and painful progress with my work. Then in the winter of 1807, when I was approaching my twenty-first birthday, it was rumored that the Cardinal Archbishop of Lyons was coming to Ecully to administer the Sacrament of Confirmation.

"You haven't been confirmed, have you, John?" asked Father Balley.

I shook my head. "No, Father. There was never the chance when I was younger, because of the Revolution."

"Well, there's the chance now. Let's pray very hard that the Holy Spirit will bring you a full measure of His seven gifts so that you can make some real progress in your work."

The Holy Spirit did bring me a goodly measure of His gifts, and I was truly grateful for them. But I could have wished for a much larger share in the Gift of Understanding. How slow I still was at books! Why, after two years of hard study, I knew no more than a boy of fourteen! Yet an even greater trial was in store for me, one which threatened to put an end to my spiritual ambitions once and for all. In the fall of 1809, when I was twenty-three years old, I received an official notice to report at once to Army Headquarters in Lyons. France was at war with both Austria and Spain. Thousands of able-bodied men were being called to the colors, including myself, John Marie Vianney.

Father Balley was beside himself at the news. "There's been some dreadful mistake!" he cried. "Why, they can't put you in the Army, John! You're a seminarian! You're free from military duties! How did your name ever get on the Army list?"

I looked at the official document which bade me report at once for training in Lyons, and shuddered. "I don't know, Father. Oh, what shall I do? This means that I have to give up the priesthood, doesn't it?"

Father Balley's face was tense. "Of course not," he said sharply. "I'll go to Lyons myself and explain things to the authorities. I'll go to see the Vicar General, too. I'll straighten everything out in just a little while, John. You'll see."

But somehow I found it hard to be encouraged. Well I knew how the Devil had been trying these many years to keep me from reaching God's altar. First there had been Father's objections. Second, those of Father Balley himself. Third, the many difficulties with my schoolwork. Now out of a clear sky came this new and truly serious obstacle.

"Things have been hard ever since I first thought of becoming a priest," I told myself wearily, glancing down at the official Army summons in my hand. "Now, though. . .oh, dear God! Are they going to be still harder?"

CHAPTER FOUR

Escape!

FATHER Balley did his best to have me excused from military service, but the authorities would not listen to him. I was not a seminarian in the strict sense of the word, they said. After all, I did not live in a seminary, but with my Aunt Marguerite and her family. Of course I attended classes at Father Balley's rectory, but then these classes were really meant for boys of twelve and fourteen—not for young men of twenty-three. Even worse, my record in these same classes was very poor and there was really not the slightest proof that I would ever be able to persevere.

"For these reasons, we can't consider your John Marie Vianney to be lawfully excused from military service," the Army authorities told Father Balley. "He must report here for training, and at once."

This news all but broke my heart. Yet even in the

midst of my grief, I asked for and received a truly
wonderful blessing: namely, the grace to realize that
everything which happens in this world can be
turned to good; that only by surrendering ourselves
to the Will of the Heavenly Father can we know
real peace.

"I'll go to Lyons, since that seems to be God's
plan for me," I told myself silently. "And I'll try very
hard not to worry or complain."

Alas! I had barely arrived in Lyons when I fell
sick and was ordered to the hospital. I stayed here
for two weeks, then was ordered to Roanne, a town
a short distance to the northwest of Lyons. But since
I was still weak, the trip was too much for me, and
when we reached Roanne I had to go to the hospital again—an up-to-date institution in the charge of
the Sisters of Saint Augustine.

"John, what a pity that they're trying to make
a soldier out of you!" exclaimed one of the Sisters
one day. "You'd be far more useful to our country
by your prayers than by going to war."

I smiled weakly. All the Sisters were spoiling me,
for they had discovered my ambition to be a priest
and knew of the mistake whereby my name had been
omitted from the list of those excused from military
service. Many in the community declared that the
government had no right to force anyone into the
Army. And there were even some who insisted that
a miracle would take place and that a certain young
student for the priesthood would never leave France
at all.

"I'm afraid that that's a bit too much to expect,"

I said. "But it would be nice, for I haven't the slightest desire to be a soldier."

Early in January, 1810, when I had been in Roanne
for six weeks, the Army authorities visited me in
the hospital and announced that I was well enough
to join my detachment, which would be leaving for
Spain on January 6. In mid-afternoon of the previous day I was to have reported at Headquarters for
detailed instructions.

"Your superior is Captain Blanchard, young man.
Here's the time of your appointment. Just be sure
that you're not late."

"I won't be late," I said.

On January 5, I bade a preliminary farewell to
my friends at the hospital and set out for Captain
Blanchard's office. Some of the Sisters were on the
verge of tears. The miracle which they had expected
had not occurred! I was really on my way to the
battlefield!

"Don't worry, Sisters," I said, with much more
confidence than I felt. "Just pray for me while I'm
gone."

Sorrowfully the good nuns agreed. "We'll pray,
John," they promised. "And not just for you, but
for your loved ones, too."

In a few minutes I was out of sight and headed
for a church some blocks distant. There was plenty
of time, I told myself, for a visit here before going
to Captain Blanchard's office.

In a little while I was kneeling before the Tabernacle and telling Our Lord of all my hopes and fears.
Was I to die on the battlefield? Oh, let me have

the grace of a truly Christian death! Was I to be
wounded? Oh, let me have the grace to suffer with
love and resignation! Was I to return home in good
health? Oh, let me have the grace to continue successfully with my studies! To be a priest someday
and help many souls to love God with all their hearts!

As I prayed, my sorrows melted away like snow
under the sun. The Heavenly Father loved me!
Someday I would be with Him forever! What else
mattered? Then after what had seemed only a few
minutes, I looked up regretfully.

"It must be time to go," I told myself.

With a last glance at the Tabernacle, I rose from
my knees and made my way slowly down the aisle
to the church door. But it needed only one look
at the winter sky for me to gasp in dismay. Twilight
was falling upon Roanne! The hour for my appointment with Captain Blanchard had long since passed!

Fear clutched my heart. "How could I have stayed
so long?" I thought. "And what about my instructions for tomorrow?"

Breathlessly I made my way to Army Headquarters, but Captain Blanchard's office was now closed.
There was nothing for me to do but to return the
next morning with an apology and an explanation.
However, when I arrived at his office the next day
the Captain was interested in neither apologies nor
explanations. It seemed that my detachment had
already set out for the Spanish frontier. There was
a war going on, and the officers in charge had had
other things to do than to wait for a lazy recruit
to report for duty.

"In church, were you?" roared the Captain. "That's a likely story!"

"But it's true, sir. And while I was praying I lost all track of the time."

The Captain glared. Then he seized me by the shoulder. "Listen, my young friend. Do you know that I have the right to throw you into prison this very minute? That deserters from the Army are dragged through the streets in chains and their families made to pay a good-sized fine?"

I began to tremble, as much from physical weakness as from fear. "Yes. . .yes, sir. I understand. But it was all a mistake. Truly it was!"

For what seemed an eternity Captain Blanchard stood towering over me, threatening this and that punishment. Then suddenly he thrust a piece of paper into my hand. "Your detachment has gone to Renaison," he snapped. "Here's the plan of march. Be off with you now and catch up with the rear guard as best you can."

Scarcely knowing what I did, I saluted and stumbled from the room. Renaison! It was several miles distant. Would I be able to reach the place before dark?

"Dear Lord, help me!" I murmured. "Holy Mother Mary, be with me on my way. . ."

There was good reason to offer these and many other fervent prayers, for I had walked only a few miles when I was forced to realize that I would not be able to catch up with my detachment. Still weak from my recent illness, I had all I could do to stumble along the highway, let alone carry a heavy pack.

The January wind was strong and bitterly cold, and soon night would be coming on.

"Perhaps if I rested awhile under those trees I could figure out what to do," I told myself. "At least, I'd be sheltered somewhat from the wind."

So I left the highway and walked a short distance through a field to a cluster of pine trees. It was much warmer here. I sat down on my pack and decided to say the Rosary while I rested. The Blessed Virgin had helped me so many times! Surely she would come to my aid again?

As I prayed, I lost all track of time. Then suddenly I heard a slight noise behind me. Turning, I saw a heavily bearded man looking at me in a kindly fashion.

"Well, young friend, and what are you doing here?"

I got to my feet, numb with cold and conscious of great weariness. "I . . . I was just resting, sir. I'm on my way to Renaison."

"_Renaison?_ Why, you'll never reach there by nightfall. Come with me. I'll find you a good place to stay." And before I could say a word, the stranger had hoisted my heavy sack to his shoulder and was on his way across the fields.

I was very tired, with no strength to ask questions. Scarcely knowing what I did, I began to follow my companion—stumbling along the rough ground and realizing only vaguely that we were headed into wild and mountainous country. But by nightfall I was truly amazed. We were now many miles from civilization, in the midst of the dense forest of Le Forez. And my new friend, who said

"I'LL FIND YOU A GOOD PLACE TO STAY."

his name was Guy, informed me that this would be a fine place to stay if I did not want to be a soldier.

"No one could possibly find you," he said. "There are several men already hiding here who don't believe that the government has the right to force any citizen to go to war."

Greatly distressed, I shook my head. "I wouldn't want to break the law. It would go too hard with my parents."

Guy laughed. "Well, we won't talk about that now. The main thing is to find a place to spend the night. Take heart, John. We're almost at the house of a friend right now."

In just a little while we came to the hut of a shoemaker, who welcomed us warmly. After eating the tasty supper prepared by his wife, we were shown to our beds and in a matter of minutes were sound asleep. But Guy awakened me very early the next morning. We must move on, he said. Through no fault of mine, I was now a deserter from the Army. If I were caught, it would mean a heavy prison sentence.

"Of course you won't be caught if you stay in these parts. No police from the city could ever make their way very far through the forest. But what worries me is this, John: you'll have to find some kind of work. And what will it be, seeing that you're not very strong?"

My head was in a whirl. I, a deserter from the Army? Oh, surely not! Why, only twenty-four hours ago I had reported to military headquarters in Roanne and done my best to obey the orders given to me!

"I can't stay here," I told Guy in a worried voice. "I've got to go on to Renaison. When I explain things..."

"Explain things? To whom? Don't you realize that your detachment left Renaison long ago? Besides, how would you find your way out of these woods?"

Hopefully I looked at my strange companion. "I thought perhaps that you..."

Guy shook his head vigorously. "Oh, no. I'm a deserter myself. There are hundreds of us up here in the forest who believe that our country has no business fighting in Spain. Or in Austria either. We're hiding out until better times come."

I could hardly believe my ears. Guy was a deserter! And then once more and with overwhelming force it struck me that I was, too. If I were caught, I could be put in chains, dragged through the streets and then sentenced to many years of hard labor. Oh, what a disgrace for my poor family! While if I remained in hiding until the war was over...if I did what my friend suggested...

For a long moment I was silent, thinking and praying. What was the best thing, THE RIGHT THING, to do? Then finally I spoke:

"Did you say that I ought to find some work?"

Guy's face brightened. "That's just what I said. Come, we'll see what we can do for you in the village of Les Noës. It's not far from here."

So it was that in a little while we presented ourselves at the house of Paul Fayot, Mayor of Les Noës. He, I was amazed to learn, was one more of the many thousands of respectable French citizens who did not believe that the government should force anyone into military life. Thus he had made himself the benefactor of several young Army deserters who were hiding out in the forest of Le Forez.

"I haven't any work for you, John," he told me kindly, "but I'm sure that my cousin Claudine will have some. She's a widow with four children. Come, I'll show you to her house."

It did not take long for Claudine Fayot—a fine Christian woman some thirty-eight years of age—to reach a decision. One look at me, still pale and thin from my recent stay in the hospital, and she declared that I might live with her until the war was over. And I could pay for my board and lodging by doing odd jobs about the farm. Maybe I could even teach her older children how to read and write. But of course we must be careful not to arouse the suspicions of the police patrols which came to the neighborhood now and then in search of Army deserters.

"John, I think that you'd better stay out of sight for the first few weeks," she decided. "And I also think that you ought to change your name. Suppose I fix a comfortable place for you in the barn? And suppose that the children and I call you . . .well, let's say *Cousin Jerome?*"

I had no objections to anything which Madame Fayot suggested. Indeed, I was overcome that the Mayor and she should treat me with so much kindness. After all, I was a complete stranger. And if they should be caught in the act of giving me shelter, it would go very hard with them. There would be a large fine and a prison sentence of at least one year.

"I'll do whatever you say," I told my new friends gratefully. "Nothing will be too hard."

Thus it was that I came to have another name—Jerome Vincent—and a new family. For Claudine Fayot treated me as though I were her own son, and her children became as dear to me as my own brothers and sisters. Then one day the two oldest boys, thirteen-year-old Louis and nine-year-old Jerome, took me aside.

"Mother told us your secret," they whispered excitedly. "We know all about your not being our real cousin, and the part about the Army, too. And we've decided to help you."

I smiled, "That's fine. And how are you going to help me?"

Louis' face was very serious. "Whenever we see the police coming, we'll give a signal—a whistle or something—and then you can run and hide in the hayloft."

Jerome nodded. "Yes. And if the police ask us questions, we'll be very stupid. We'll pretend that we don't understand a word they're saying."

I thanked my young friends for their offer of help, and we agreed upon a signal in the event that the police should come—a long, low whistle, repeated several times. Then an opening into the hayloft was made, just above the rack from which the cattle fed, so that in an emergency it would be easy for me to rush into the cattle pen, swing myself up through this hole into the loft, then cover myself with hay.

"Only let's hope that I never have to do this," I thought fervently. "It would be too close a call."

For several months all went well. I did odd jobs about the Fayot farm and taught the children Catechism, reading and writing. Then one hot summer day while I was working in the fields I heard a long, low whistle, followed by another and yet another. Looking up, I saw two policemen coming slowly down the road in the direction of Claudine Fayot's house. In the background, Louis and Jerome were signalling frantically.

My heart in my mouth, I dropped my hoe and raced for the barn. Quickly I swung myself up through the hole above the feed rack into the loft overhead. The hay! I must burrow into it like an animal! I must cover myself with it and lie as still as a mouse! Yet even as I did so, my blood ran cold. The policemen had quickened their steps and now were in the yard below! And they were shouting angry threats at the entire household!

I groaned. "Those men must have seen me come up here," I told myself, trembling. "Oh, dear Blessed Mother! What's going to happen now?"

CHAPTER FIVE

A New Decision

THERE was not long to wait. The policemen insisted that an Army deserter was hiding somewhere about the Fayot property. They would not go until they had found him. And they would begin their search in the barn.

Suddenly I felt that my time had truly come. How hot it was under the suffocating pile of hay! Why, I could scarcely breathe! And how hard to remain perfectly still! Yet soon I discovered that the agony was just beginning. The policemen announced that they were going to do a thorough job of searching. If the task took an hour, two hours, all afternoon, what of it? There was plenty of time. Besides, it was much too hot to hurry.

For what seemed an eternity the search went on. Finally the two officials, sword in hand, clambered into the dimly-lighted loft and began to poke about in the hay. In the stifling depths of my hiding place I offered a quick prayer:

"Dear Lord, if You'll just let these men pass by, I promise that never again during my whole life will I complain about anything. . .no matter how hard it is!"

One minute! Two minutes! Three minutes! Suddenly one of the policemen dipped his sword into the very bundle of hay beneath which I was lying. Desperately I gritted my teeth. I must not move, I must not breathe, or all would be lost. But, oh, thanks be to God, suddenly my little prayer of a few minutes before was answered! The sword stopped short of my body.

"I've had enough of this wild-goose chase," said the officer, kicking over a box in his disgust. "Let's go over to the Mayor's house and have something to eat."

"That's the first sensible idea you've had today," replied his companion. "Come on."

Naturally there was great rejoicing in the Fayot household that night over the policemen's failure to discover my whereabouts. Yet somehow my heart was heavy. Here I was, hunted like a criminal, getting older and making absolutely no progress toward the priesthood. . .

As we sat together in the cool of the evening, Claudine Fayot seemed to read my thoughts. "You're not really happy with us, are you, Jerome?"

I hesitated. "Oh, yes! You're so good to me! But if I could be back in Ecully with Father Balley. . .if I could be working at my books. . ."

THEY BEGAN TO POKE ABOUT IN THE HAY.

"You still want to be a priest?"

"More than anything in the world!"

"It will mean suffering, my son. Lots more suffering."

"I know. But surely the priesthood is worth *any* suffering, no matter how great?"

For a long moment Claudine Fayot looked at me, love and sympathy shining from her eyes. Then she stretched out a motherly hand. "Of course it is," she said. "And don't worry. You'll be going back to Father Balley one of these days. I just know you will."

My benefactress was right. Within a few weeks word arrived through secret channels that back in Dardilly my youngest brother had enlisted in the Army. And because he had done this voluntarily, and far before his time, I could return home without fear of being forced into military service. He had taken my place, so to speak. Even more. France was now at peace. All deserters, including myself, had been issued a general pardon.

How my heart sang at the news! I was free! Free to look any man in the eye, to come and go as I pleased, to return to my studies for the priesthood! Yet the entire Fayot household was plunged into gloom. Soon "Cousin Jerome" would be going away! Soon there would be no more lessons in reading and writing and Catechism!

"I don't know what we'll do without you," Madame Fayot told me tearfully. "You've been such a help around the farm. Now—why, it'll be almost as though you were dead. Oh, Jerome—I mean John—how are we going to bear it?"

I comforted my "second mother" as best I could.
There would be visits, I suggested. And letters. After
all, Les Noës was not so very far from Ecully. Then
suddenly Madame Fayot looked at me intently.

"I know, John! Someday you'll come back and be
our parish priest! That's what'll happen. And it'll
settle everything. Oh, how wonderful!"

I smiled at the childlike trust and enthusiasm.
"It would be wonderful," I agreed. "And maybe the
Heavenly Father will let things work out that way."

But there was little time for idle thought about
the future, and soon I was making joyful preparations for my return home. What an eternity since
I had seen my parents, my brothers, my sister
Gothon! Yet in the end I deferred my going for
several months. The reason? I wished to be of some
use to the Fayot family during the time of harvest.
And when that was over I busied myself at odd jobs
about the farm that needed a man's touch. Finally,
though, the hour for departure did arrive—on a cold
day in January of the year 1811.

"You'll come back, John?" pleaded Claudine Fayot,
her children, the Mayor and dozens of other good
friends I had made.

I nodded, hard-pressed to keep my feelings under
control. "Of course I'll come back! Why, this is just
like home to me! Oh, how can I thank you for everything that you've done?"

Thus it was that I took leave of Les Noës, not
realizing that the long-dreamed-of return to my
father's farm at Dardilly and to Father Balley's classes
in Ecully would be marred by a great sorrow. Yet

scarcely two weeks after my arrival, death claimed the best friend I had in all the world—my mother. At once friends and neighbors for miles around hastened to console me. "Your mother was a saint, John," one old woman declared earnestly. "I just know that she went straight to Heaven."

"Yes," insisted another. "And I can tell you how she became a saint: by always doing little things well."

Listening to these and other loyal tributes, I was deeply touched. Oh, I must not grieve unduly! Mother's death so soon after my return from sixteen months of exile was part of God's all-wise plan for her, and for me. Yet more than once I found my heart growing heavy and forlorn. For years Mother had done everything possible to help me attain to the priesthood. What prayers! What sacrifices! What boundless confidence in my ability to reach the goal! And now she was gone. . .she would never even have the chance to see me at the altar. . .

In the end it was Father Balley who came to my aid, and with truly inspired words.

"Your mother hasn't really gone," he said kindly. "Why, this very minute she is better able and more eager to help you than she ever was on earth."

I stared in amazement. "You don't mean. . ."

"I mean that your mother is now one of the perfect souls in Heaven. And being perfect, she really understands the value of the wonderful gift God has offered you in calling you to the priesthood. Oh, John! Why not ask her to obtain the many graces you need in order to be ordained a priest? Why waste any more time in idle grief?"

So it was that I took fresh courage, and daily addressed a petition to my mother for success in my work. I was now just a little short of my twenty-fifth birthday. Surely she would see to it that I completed my studies without any more delay?

Father Balley joined his prayers to mine, and as the months passed I realized gratefully that I was doing a little better in Latin. Another joy was also mine. Now I no longer lived with Aunt Marguerite and her family, but at the rectory in the capacity of sacristan and handyman—a real privilege, since it gave me the chance to observe Father Balley at close range. What a saint he was! How mortified in every way! Truly, he had died to all the vanities of the world and now had only one aim in life—to do the Will of the Heavenly Father with the same spirit of love and abandonment as Christ had done it on earth.

"That's the only way to be really happy," he often told me, "to have no will of one's own, but only the Will of the Eternal Father."

I pondered these words very often, and presently an urge to follow closely in Father Balley's footsteps grew strong within me. Did he perform a certain act of mortification in order to weaken any tendency to do his own will instead of God's Will? Then with his permission I would peform the same mortification. By constant effort to know, love and do the Will of God I would try to be a saint, too.

Father Balley was well pleased with my ambition. "There's just one thing to remember," he said, smiling slightly.

"What, Father?"

"That God's Will for us goes on and on until we draw our last breath. When we think of it thus, of all the trials and struggles to keep faithful to it, we might well lose courage. But we mustn't think of it in this way, John."

"No, Father?"

"No. We must think of God's Will only as it applies to the present second, the present minute, the present hour, and be completely abandoned to it. Then certainly the future will take care of itself."

I tried to keep these words always before me, particularly during the autumn days of the year 1812. For at this time I left Father Balley's rectory to enter the Minor Seminary at Verrières. Some two hundred young men were enrolled here for the purpose of studying philosophy. After one year of successful work, each of us would be entitled to apply for admission to the Major Seminary in Lyons.

I found the studies at Verrières extremely difficult, and there was much teasing on the part of my companions because I was older than the professor who had charge of our class. Before many weeks had passed, however, I had left this class and had taken my place in a special section of seven students. The sole distinction of this little group was that no one in it knew enough Latin to keep abreast of the regular schedule.

"How these boys ever expect to become priests is beyond me," sighed the Rector. "Perhaps coaching will help. But a miracle would be even better!"

The Father Rector did not exaggerate. We seven

were very slow at books, and I—the oldest—was the slowest of all. In June, 1813, when the year's reports were given out, mine was not at all encouraging. In fact, it was downright disappointing.

Application . . . . Good
General knowledge . . . . Very weak
Conduct . . . . Good
Character . . . . Good

Yet harder times were coming. When I entered the Major Seminary in Lyons in October of that same year, I learned to my keen distress that there would be no special classes here for backward students. A boy who could not understand the Latin lectures was held to have no business being on hand. And in the classroom the professors spoke only in Latin and expected their students to reply in the same language.

"I can read a little Latin, if I have plenty of time to figure it out," I told Father Mioland, one of the professors, "but I can't understand a word when it's spoken. Oh, what am I going to do, Father? All the lectures are being wasted on me, and there's no way that I can learn anything!"

Father Mioland was a kind man. "Maybe I could help you," he suggested. And for several weeks he did give me private lessons in Latin and philosophy. A brilliant fellow-student, John Duplay, also coached me in Latin. But at Easter of the year 1814, after I had been in the Major Seminary some six months, the dreaded blow fell. The Father Rector called me to his office and announced that he did not believe that I had a vocation to the priesthood.

"You'd better go home, my son," he told me kindly. "You're just wasting our time and yours by staying here."

I made no effort to plead my cause with the Father Rector. Nor did I let anyone know my great grief in being dismissed from the Major Seminary. Yet it took all my faith in God's loving designs for me not to give in to despair. What a disgrace to be sent home for failure in studies at the age of twenty-eight!

"But you mustn't give up hope, John!" whispered a confident little voice in my heart. *"Go and see Father Balley. He'll help you as he's always helped before."*

I would not listen to the little voice, however. Already, I decided, I had bothered Father Balley too much. It was high time that I learned to stand upon my own two feet.

"Perhaps I could be a Brother somewhere," I thought wearily. "Perhaps I could give myself to God's service after all, only in a different way from what I planned..."

The more I pondered the idea, the better it seemed. Brothers did not have to know Latin. All they had to do was to work with their hands, to be humble and obedient, prayerful and mortified.

Suddenly all was quite clear. I would go to the Brothers of Christian Doctrine in Lyons. Surely they would be able to find a place for me—in the kitchen or barn or somewhere...

CHAPTER SIX

A FRIEND of my childhood days, one John Dumond, recently had received the habit at the Brothers' novitiate house in Lyons. Without more ado I decided to go and see him. It would be interesting to hear what he had to say about the religious life.

I found my friend—now Brother Gerard—highly enthusiastic. "Oh, it's wonderful to be part of a community!" he exclaimed. "I'm sure that you'd be quite happy here, John. Everyone is so kind. And the work—well, I never thought I'd find any work so interesting as that which I've been given to do. Why don't you come and join our little family?"

Hesitantly I outlined my plan. I would like to be a Brother—if the superiors would have me. First, though, it seemed best to go to Ecully to see Father Balley; then to Dardilly to see my family. After that, if all went well...

"Of course all will go well," Brother Gerard assured me confidently. "As long as a candidate has good health and a good intention, there's nothing for him to worry about. Oh, John! I'm so happy that you want to come here!"

Father Balley was of a different opinion, however. When he first heard about my decision to become a Brother, he looked at me sadly. Then suddenly his expression changed and in emphatic tones he declared that I was about to make a dreadful mistake. "Write at once to your friend in Lyons not to breathe a word of what you told him," he ordered. "Say that I want you to go on with your studies for the priesthood."

I could hardly believe my ears. "But I've been dismissed from the Seminary, Father! How can I ever hope to be a priest now?"

Father Balley's eyes met mine unflinchingly. "How? Why, I'll teach you myself, of course."

Then slowly and calmly, as though to a child, my good friend began to speak his mind. I had commenced my studies for the priesthood at the age of nineteen. Nine years had passed, and all during that time I had worked very hard to achieve my goal. But the Devil must have worked still harder, for now that I was twenty-eight years old he was the one to be succeeding, not I.

"Of course you know, John, that one of the Devil's really important activities is to keep you—and other young men like you—from the priesthood?"

I nodded miserably. "Yes, Father."

"And so you've decided to give in to him."

I started back in dismay. "Oh, no!"

"But you just told me that you were through with your studies, that you were going to be a Brother and not worry any more about books!"

I twisted my hands nervously. "That isn't giving in to the Devil, is it, Father?"

"For some it wouldn't be, John. It would be a fine and wonderful thing, a giving in to the grace of God. But for you—well, I'm afraid that it's just a lazy way out of an unpleasant situation."

As I sat there, now anxious and depressed beyond words, Father Balley continued to talk in slow and confident tones. An idea had just occurred to him, he said. This was to teach me (but certainly never in Latin!) what my friends in Lyons would be learning in their classrooms during the next three months. Surely renewed prayer and sacrifice would see to it that at the end of May, when the time for final examinations came, I would go back to the Seminary with sufficient knowledge to pass in each subject. Then what could the professors do, when the Bishop came in July, but send me on with the other students to receive Minor Orders—perhaps even to be made a subdeacon?

"It's all so very simple, and therefore just what the Devil doesn't expect, John. Aren't you willing to try again?"

I looked in amazement at my good friend and teacher. What a saint he was! How much time and effort and prayers and sufferings he had offered to God in my behalf! And he was willing to sacrifice

"YOU'VE DECIDED TO GIVE IN TO THE DEVIL?"

himself still further. . .

I took a deep breath. "All right," I whispered. "I'll try again. But oh, Father! If I ever am a priest, it'll only be because of you!"

So it was that I took up my studies once more, and three months later returned to the Seminary for the final examinations. But as I came before the examining board, pale-faced and trembling, what little knowledge I had had of each subject promptly left me. How dreadful to have to face the most learned and distinguished priests of the Archdiocese—and without a sensible thought in my head! Oh, surely they were all thinking the same thing: that never had there been such a stupid candidate for Minor Orders as John Marie Vianney! Why, he could not understand the simplest question when it was put to him in Latin, let alone give a satisfactory answer! Who was he, anyway? And what had ever made him think that he could be a priest?

Naturally there was only one result of the oral examinations at the Seminary: *complete failure!* Yet the following day Father Balley went to Lyons and made one last and valiant effort in my behalf.

"Through nervousness my poor son lost his head at the examinations," he told the Vicar General, Monsignor Courbon, who had been one of the examiners. "Oh, Monsignor! If you could give John just one more chance! If you and some of the others could come to Ecully and give him another examination in my rectory. . .among familiar surroundings where he'd feel more at ease. . ."

The Vicar General had a very high opinion of

Father Balley. Now, though, he looked at him a trifle curiously.

"This is a most irregular request, Father."

"I know it, Monsignor."

"John Marie Vianney has an extremely poor record as a student."

"I know that, too."

"Yet you think that he'd make a good priest?"

"Oh, I'm sure of it!"

"Well, of course I can promise nothing, Father. But I'll see what I can do about coming to Ecully."

Just twenty-four hours later the Vicar General did come, and accompanied by two learned priests. My heart was pounding like a trip hammer as Father Balley brought me forward to meet the distinguished visitors. But these greeted me so kindly that almost at once my fear melted away. A little later each asked me a few simple questions, which I managed to answer correctly. Then the Vicar General turned to Father Balley.

"Is this young man fond of prayer, Father?"

"Oh, yes, Monsignor."

"Has he a devotion to Our Lady?"

"Since early childhood."

"He knows how to say the Rosary?"

"Yes, he is a model of piety."

There was a long pause, and once again my heart began to pound. The Vicar General's eyes were lowered, his lips moving. Obviously he was praying for enlightenment, since in his hands—with the Cardinal Archbishop of Lyons not at home—rested my fate. *Was God really calling me to the priesthood?*

Suddenly the good man turned to me. His eyes were very kind. "A model of piety? Splendid! I summon this young man to come up for Ordination. The grace of God will do the rest."

What joy and happiness now were mine! At last my goal was in sight, and for the rest of the day I kept repeating to myself, in an unbelieving whisper, the Vicar General's wonderful words. Then in a few weeks my happiness grew even more intense. On July 2, through a special dispensation, I received the four Minor Orders and was ordained a subdeacon!

"Oh, dear Lord, now I really do belong to Your service!" I told myself, hardly able to realize the thrilling truth. "Now I really am going to be a priest..."

Even though I had been raised to the dignity of the subdiaconate, however, much more study was required before I could progress. But I did not return to the Seminary for this study. Because of my former failure there, it was thought best that Father Balley should take charge of my education. So I continued to reside with him at the rectory as sacristan and general helper—spending several hours each day in reading and studying.

Of course I had always known that my good friend was an excellent instructor, kind and patient and thorough. After all, what other kind of tutor could possibly have succeeded with me? But during the next year I learned one thing from him that was not actually contained in those textbooks which he sent me to master—namely, that to be successful in his work, a priest must be willing to pray and suffer for souls every day of his life.

"What a pity that so many pastors don't understand this!" my teacher told me more than once. "But it's true, John. The conversion of sinners begins with prayer and ends with penance. Remember this when you go out to win souls from sin."

I considered this saying very often, especially as it might be applied to France. For after the horrors of the Revolution and the hardships of war, our country was in a truly dreadful condition. Most of the political leaders declared that success was to be measured only in terms of wealth, power or worldly knowledge. Millions of people agreed with them, so that now religion had come to mean almost nothing. Indeed, ignorance and vice were flourishing in both town and countryside, and few and far between were those men and women who knelt each day to ask God's blessing upon themselves, their families, their work. But, I reflected, suppose that one pastor would set himself to pray for the sinners and the lukewarm souls who lived within his parish and do penance for them, *real penance?* And suppose that he could find two or three of his flock willing to do the same?

"The Heavenly Father would surely be touched by so much prayer and sacrifice," I decided. "He would see to it that the sinners in that parish were converted, the lukewarm souls filled with zeal and one little corner of France made really holy."

One little corner of France! It sounded very small and unimportant, yet somehow I glimpsed the wonder of it all. Oh, what a truly marvelous work awaited even the most obscure pastor who was not afraid to spend himself for souls! Not only could he bring real peace and joy to human hearts, but he could also make saints out of those about him...out of ordinary men and women...boys and girls...

"Father Balley isn't afraid to do good by praying and suffering for others," I thought. "Oh, dear Lord, couldn't You let me become just a little bit like him? And couldn't You let many other priests want to be like him, too? Then surely the world would be a much better place..."

The months passed, and on June 23, 1815, I was ordained a deacon at the Cathedral of Saint John in Lyons. How my heart overflowed with happiness! Yet in a few weeks this happiness was completely overshadowed. At this time I underwent another examination in Father Balley's rectory before Canon Bochard, a learned priest of the Archdiocese of Lyons, and was informed that I might present myself for Ordination to the priesthood on August 9 at the Major Seminary in Grenoble.

"You've made good progress this last year, John," said the Canon approvingly. "I'm really pleased with you."

I clasped my hands eagerly. "Oh, I'm so glad, Canon! I worked as hard as I could."

But when I went to the Vicar General's office to receive the necessary papers to take with me to Grenoble, there was a real disappointment. True enough, I was to be ordained a priest on August 9. From then until the hour of my death I would have the wonderful power to turn ordinary bread and wine into the Body and Blood of Christ. But, declared the authorities, there was one important priestly function that I was not fitted to perform.

"We can't let you hear Confessions, John," said the Vicar General kindly. "You. . .well, I guess you know why."

I nodded miserably. "Yes, Monsignor. I'm too stupid."

"Don't put it that way, my son. Say, rather, that you're not prepared for the work because you never studied the required texts. And don't feel too bad. Of course the Church needs learned priests, yet she needs other priests, too. Do you know what kind I mean?"

I hesitated so long that in the end the Vicar General had to supply the answer to his own question. "John, the Church needs holy priests," he said gravely, *"holy priests above all things!"*

Suddenly a wave of longing swept my heart. I was dreadfully stupid, of course. Never, never could I be a learned priest. But perhaps—oh, happy thought! —I could be a holy one?

CHAPTER SEVEN

THE most glorious day of my life finally arrived—August 13, 1815. Then, within the somber walls of the Major Seminary in Grenoble, and at the age of twenty-nine years and three months, I received the greatest honor a man can know in this world. I became, not king or president or millionaire, but priest—another Christ, with the privilege of offering sacrifice to the Heavenly Father each day and receiving in return the most wonderful blessings for myself and for others!

"Dear God, I'd like to be a really holy priest!" I whispered softly, just before beginning my first Mass. "I'd like to save many souls for Heaven! Won't You please help me to do these things?"

Later, when I considered the question of souls, I wondered where I would be sent to work for them. Perhaps to Les Noës, the little village in the forest of Le Forez near which I had taken refuge with the Fayot family five years ago? Already I had written to the pastor there, offering my services as an assistant. Yet upon my return to Ecully I found that other arrangements had been made.

"John, I've been given an assistant!" cried Father Balley joyfully. "And it's you, my son! It's you! Oh, how splendid!"

I was really touched at the childlike happiness of my loyal friend and teacher. He, saint that he was, had never wanted me to go to Les Noës. Or anyplace else. He had wanted me to stay with him. And this despite all the suffering and embarrassment which I had caused by being so slow at books.

"I'll do everything I can to be of help here, Father," I said gratefully. "Truly I will!"

Thus it was that I began my duties as assistant in Ecully during the summer of 1815—my first pastoral act being a Baptism performed on August 27. But very soon I found myself in an awkward situation. Because I had spent so many years in Ecully, first at my Aunt Marguerite's house as a student, later at the rectory as sacristan and handyman, I had made several friends. Now these came to me and asked me to look after their souls: to hear their Confessions and give them spiritual advice.

"But I can't hear Confessions," I announced regretfully. "You'll have to go to Father Balley as usual."

My friends were amazed. What kind of a priest was I, not to be able to hear Confessions? So very briefly I tried to explain matters.

"I haven't studied enough," I said.

Tactfully my friends refrained from asking more questions, although I could tell that they were really puzzled. *I hadn't studied enough?* they seemed to be saying. *Well, why not? For years Father Balley had spent himself in my regard, slaving long hours over this and that book. Now that I was ordained, he had probably arranged that I should pay him back for his goodness by acting as his assistant. But actually how much assistance did I give? Of course every morning I offered Mass in the parish church: occassionally I preached a short sermon on Sundays; I helped out a little with Catechism lessons, too. But surely Father Balley was doing just about as much work as ever—and he sixty-four years of age?*

Sensing such thoughts, I decided upon a frank statement. "I believe that your good pastor took me to live with him out of the kindness of his heart, and because no one else would have me," I declared. "Oh, let's pray very hard that he won't have to suffer too much. . ."

The months passed, and I did what I could for the people of Ecully. Some days I took Holy Communion to the sick. On others, I gathered the children about me and told them stories of God and of the saints. More generally, though, I accompanied Father Balley on visits about the parish, listening with love and reverence as he advised and encouraged the various members of his flock.

There were also occasional trips outside the parish. Sometimes these were to Tassin, a splendid country estate which belonged to Anthony Jaricot, a

"PLEASE LET ME BRING YOU MANY SOULS!"

wealthy manufacturer of Lyons. Here I had the privilege of meeting one of the Jaricot daughters—
sixteen-year-old Pauline—a beautiful and talented
girl who, although no one guessed it then, one day
would establish the Society for the Propagation of
the Faith. Again, Father Balley sometimes took me
into the city of Lyons to visit certain people who
were his friends. And of course there were the many
hours we spent together at the rectory over books,
for the good man would not let me rest from my
studies. The reason? It was all made clear when an
important paper arrived one day from the Vicar
General's office in Lyons.

"John, here's some news that seems to concern
you," said my friend and teacher, smiling just a little. "I suppose you can guess what it is?"

I shook my head. "No, Father. I haven't the slightest idea."

"Why, you can now hear Confessions—either here
in Ecully or anywhere else in the Archdiocese!"

My heart gave a great leap. *I could hear Confessions?* Oh, surely not! Yet Father Balley repeated
that it was so. Several months had passed since my
Ordination, and during that time I had gained considerable priestly experience. Even more, I had kept
at my books, mastering much new material. Recently
the Vicar General had been assured that I now knew
enough to be able to render correct decisions in
the confessional.

"So here's the document you've been lacking so
long, John. Oh, my son! How much good you'll be
able to do now!"

I took the document in trembling fingers. What an enormous responsibility was suddenly mine! To listen to the sins of my fellowmen as though I were God Himself; to advise, to warn, to help, to encourage; to make sure that every grave sin was mentioned; that the penitent made a real effort to be sorry for his sins; that he was resolved that, using the graces God would give him, he would never fall into serious sin again. Then finally, with the sublime words of Absolution upon my tongue, to release the heavenly power that was in me by reason of the priesthood and wash away all guilt and stain from the sinner's soul...

Suddenly I turned, and my heart gave another great leap. Without warning Father Balley had gotten to his knees before me!

"Bless me, Father, for I have sinned," he was saying humbly. "Will you hear my Confession, please?"

It was almost too much. My saintly friend and teacher kneeling before *me*...about to tell *me* his few human failings! Yet even as the thought struck home, another took its place. Father Balley was not kneeling before *me*. He was kneeling before Christ *in* me. Slow and stupid though I was, the grace of God had yet made me a priest and now I was privileged to hear Confessions as much as any Cardinal or Archbishop—or the Pope himself.

"All right, Father," I said. "I'll gladly hear your Confession."

Naturally it was soon common knowledge that I was "approved" for hearing Confessions. As a result, I finally became of real use to Father Balley as assistant pastor—with scarcely a day passing when I did not help one or more souls to make their peace with God. But while I listened to the sins of others, I well knew my own frailty. Thus, one day I decided to make something of a bargain with the Blessed Mother. Every day for the rest of my life I would say certain prayers in her honor. In return, she would obtain for me the grace of purity. And what prayers should I say? Why, the *Regina Coeli* (which takes the place of the Angelus during Paschaltide) and an ejaculation: *"Blessed be forever the Most Holy and Immaculate Conception of the Blessed Virgin Mary, Mother of God. Amen."*

"I'll say the *Regina Coeli* once and the ejaculation six times each day," I told myself. "Surely the Blessed Mother will be pleased, and will give me the great grace of a pure life?"

So the days passed. I prayed and worked to the best of my ability, taking Father Balley as my constant model. For the man was such a saint! Why, if the world's greatest sinner could hear him utter his favorite ejaculation: *"My God, I love Thee with my whole heart!"* surely he would be converted?

Yet these peaceful days which I had known since Ordination were fast drawing to a close. Early in the year 1817 Father Balley fell ill. A painful ulcer developed on one leg, and finally he was forced to take to his bed. On December 17, after I had heard his Confession and administered the Last Rites, he gave up his soul to God.

What sorrow for me now! What heartbreak! My best friend was gone—he, who more than anyone else had made it possible for me to be a priest! Oh, what would I do? Where would I go?

"Why, you'll stay here with us, Father," everyone in Ecully insisted. "You'll be our pastor, and someone else will be assistant."

I thanked my good friends for their offer, but hastened to explain that I was too inexperienced for such a work. After all, Ecully was a good-sized town and the pastor's duties very numerous. I would do far better in a less responsible post.

"Perhaps in Les Noës," I told myself hopefully, my thoughts returning once more to the little village in the forest of Le Forez that had given me hospitality so many years ago. Surely there would be work for me here—if not as pastor, at least as assistant? And how good to see my many friends again. . .Claudine Fayot and her children . . . the Mayor and his wife. . .the shoemaker. . .the blacksmith. . .

But the Vicar General had made other arrangements, sending one Father Tripler to Ecully to be pastor and appointing me to continue as assistant. Then two months later, in February, 1818, I was informed that my days in Ecully were over. I was to go, not to Les Noës, but to Ars—an obscure village some nineteen miles distant—where I would serve as the curé, or parish priest.

"There's not much love of God in Ars, Father," said the Vicar General regretfully. "You must bring some into it."

I nodded gravely. "I'll try, Monsignor."

"Good. And plan to leave within a week or so. The sooner you get started with this new work, you know, the better."

I agreed. Early in the morning of February 9, I set out on foot for Ars. A good woman of Ecully, one Madame Bibost, accompanied me. She was a widow and had finally persuaded me that I would need a housekeeper at Ars, and that she would be able to do better in that capacity than anyone else. After all, hadn't she known me since my boyhood days? Didn't she understand just how I liked things done?

It was an uneventful walk from Ecully to Ars, through rather uninteresting countryside. There were no forests or hills, and the road was full of holes. Smiling, I recalled what I had once heard somebody say—that this part of the Archdiocese of Lyons was so deserted and forlorn that only those priests who gave no promise of amounting to anything were sent here to be pastors or assistants.

"I'm glad that Ars is just a little place," I thought. "I'll be able to get to know everyone very well."

But as the hours passed and it grew late in the afternoon, both Madame Bibost and I wished that Ars were a really important place. For where was it, anyway? No one we met in our travels seemed to know. Finally a thick mist began to creep across the fields, and with sinking hearts we realized that the winter's day was almost over. Soon it would be night. Then what should we do?

Suddenly Madame Bibost tugged at my sleeve. "There are some little shepherds over in that field, Father," she said eagerly, pointing through the mist. "Perhaps they'll know where the place is."

I called to the group of children, and slowly they

came over to the roadside—their eyes wide with curiosity at the sight of two strangers. But as the minutes passed, never a word would they say in response to our earnest questioning as to the whereabouts of Ars.

"What stupid children!" exclaimed Madame Bibost finally. "Why, they can't even open their mouths!"

I smiled. "I don't think they're stupid. It's just that they can't understand us because they know only their own peasant dialect."

For a long moment Madame Bibost and I stood there in the road, staring over the children's heads at the gloomy landscape and wondering what to do. Then one of the boys made a shy gesture. "Ars?" he said.

I turned in amazement, then nodded encouragingly. "Yes, little friend. Ars. Where is it? Do you know?"

The boy pointed down the road, while in halting phrases he made us understand that the village, hidden in the thick mist, was only a little distance away and that we were now standing on the spot which marked the boundary of the parish. Then he added that his name was Anthony—Anthony Givre.

At once the heaviness vanished from my heart. "Anthony, you've shown me the way to Ars," I said gratefully. "I'll show you the way to Heaven." Then, moved by an impulse of grace, I knelt down on the spot that marked the boundary of my parish.

"Heavenly Father, please let me do good work here!" I begged. "Please let me bring You many souls!"

There was no time for lengthy prayer, however. Accompanied by the children, Madame Bibost and I set off down the road. In just a few minutes we glimpsed some scattered huts in the midst of which stood a dilapidated church. The low, thatched cottages looked thoroughly depressing in the gathering gloom.

"How small it all is!" I exclaimed. Yet even as I spoke, a strange conviction filled my soul. Ars was small, yes. And poor and abandoned. But someday it would be great. It would not be able to hold all those who would come to it. Why? How? I did not know. But surely it would happen thus.

CHAPTER EIGHT

Sowing the Seed

IN JUST a few days I realized how truly the Vicar General had spoken when he had said that there was not much love of God in Ars. Out of the two hundred and thirty people living there, less than a score went to Mass on Sundays. And the four taverns in the village were the centers for drunkenness and gambling. Then I discovered that children and grown-ups alike were addicted to cursing and swearing and the use of coarse language, and that hardly anyone bothered to keep holy the Lord's Day, but would do servile work in the fields or at home on the slightest provocation.

"The people aren't really bad, though," I tried to reassure myself. "They're just ignorant. After all, many of them grew up during the Revolution and so never had any religious training."

But at the end of my first week in Ars I felt almost

overcome. What a lot of work there was to be done in my little parish! For instance, there was no school, and even among the older folk hardly anyone knew how to read or write. Neither were there any Catechism lessons for the children. As for the young men and women, their one great interest seemed to be the village dances, rowdy affairs which lasted far into the night and which were frequently the occasion of serious sin. Certainly it was evident that, save for five or six pious families, no one in Ars was in the habit of considering the real reason why he or she had been born: namely, to know, love and serve God in this world and then be happy with Him forever in the next.

"Well, things simply must change," I told myself emphatically. "Otherwise, how can anyone in this poor little village hope to save his soul?"

But how were things to change? I was not quite thirty-two years old—shy, awkward and without any real experience in administering the affairs of a parish. How could I work what would amount to a miracle and make each member of my flock truly conscious of death, Judgment, Heaven, Hell? How was I to impress upon each one that nothing matters in this world save learning to mold our wills according to the Will of God, so that we no longer wish for anything save what He permits to happen to us during each minute of the day? And what could I do about the missing of Mass and the unnecessary servile work on Sundays? The drinking and the gambling in the village taverns? The cursing and the swearing? The rowdy and immoral dances?

"Of myself I can't do a thing," I decided. "But it can be really different if I offer prayer and sacrifice to the Heavenly Father, uniting them to the merits of Christ's sufferings and death upon the Cross."

And what sacrifices would I offer to the Heavenly Father for the conversion of my people? Ah, there were so many things that I could do! But in my opinion there was one sacrifice that stood out above all others. This was fasting. Hadn't Christ Himself fasted, later explaining to the Apostles what a wonderful power this practice has to loosen the Devil's grip upon souls, particularly those addicted to the sins of impurity? Well, I would try to make this valuable mortification my own, too.

"Beginning right now, I'll take less to eat and drink each day," I told myself. "Oh, Father in Heaven! Please let this sacrifice bring graces to my parish!"

But when I explained about the fasting to Madame Bibost, declaring that now it would not be necessary for her to remain with me as cook and housekeeper, she was beside herself with dismay.

"You're going to fast every day?" she cried in horrified tones. "Why, you'll kill yourself, Father! Other priests don't do that for their people."

"Perhaps not. But do they make saints out of them?"

"Well . . ."

"My good friend, that is all I want: to make saints here in this little corner of France."

"Yes, but there must be some other way than by suffering, Father!"

I smiled at the worried expression on poor Madame Bibost's face. "No," I said gently. "If the people in a parish are to love God, *really love Him,* the priests in charge must prepare the way by doing penance."

A few days later my would-be housekeeper went back to Ecully, uttering dire prophecies. I was going to kill myself, she said, even though her good friend Madame Renard had promised to keep an eye on me. Fasting! That might be all right for monks and nuns and hermits, but hardly for a busy parish priest. And surely I would make many enemies in Ars if I tried to change the local customs?

One of Madame Bibost's fears was soon justified. There was hard feeling in Ars when I preached on the evils which had taken root in people's hearts. The tavern-keepers in particular resented my words.

"If Father Vianney doesn't like to drink and gamble, that's all right," they said. "He's a priest. But why does he try to spoil other people's fun and our business? Is that what it means to be a Christian?"

In their turn, the young people grew almost as indignant as the tavern-keepers. Although they respected me because I was a priest, they decided that I was narrow-minded and old-fashioned beyond words. I wanted to stop their dancing on the village green, even in their homes when there was a wedding or a christening or some other cause for celebration!

"If he could, our new pastor would keep us in church all day," they grumbled. "As though there were any fun in *that!*"

I was hurt and disappointed. Everything I had said about the taverns was true. Men drank to excess there, blasphemed, squandered their wages and completely forgot their duties to wives and children. As for the dances—how could I approve of them when they caused so many young people to fall into serious sin?

"I can't back down on what I've said," I told myself, "and I won't. But oh, Heavenly Father! Please help me to show my people that I do love them, that I want them to be really happy, and that the only happiness that counts—no matter how hard this is to believe at first—is that which is to be found in becoming holy!"

But while I prayed and made sacrifices for the conversion of Ars, it was a consolation to remember that the little village was not completely without its good Christians. For instance, Anthony Mandy and Michael Cinier, mayor and councillor, respectively, were God-fearing men and my friends from the start. Then there was a really devout and cultured lady, Mademoiselle Marie Anne des Garets, who lived in her family's ancestral castle on the outskirts of the village.

"Father, I'll do everything that I can to help you in your work," she told me, shortly after my arrival. "Just what are your plans?"

Very willingly I began to outline them. I wanted the people of Ars to be God-centered instead of self-centered. I wanted them to come to Mass each Sunday, not to work in the fields or to profane the Lord's Day by drinking and gambling in the taverns. I

wanted the children to be taught Catechism. I
wanted the swearing and the cursing to stop, as well
as the sinful dances. I wanted a school to be opened.
I wanted to establish the Confraternity of the Rosary
for women and girls and the Guild of the Blessed
Sacrament for men and boys. I wanted to repair the
church, which was so poor and dilapidated as to
be a disgrace, even a public hazard.

Mademoiselle Marie Anne was sixty-four years of
age, twice as old as I. As I stood before her, eagerly
outlining my plans for the future, she kept smiling
and nodding sympathetically.

"I'm sure that you'll do all these things, and even
more, Father. But it would be a big mistake to
attempt everything at once. So which of these plans
do you think you'll try first?"

It was hard to make a choice, of course, but finally
I decided to concentrate upon the children. Yes, I
would start a class in Catechism for the boys and
girls of Ars. And it would meet not just on Sundays,
but every day of the week. I would do my best to
make the little ones understand that the most important work they would ever have to do in this life
would be to make themselves holy and pleasing to
God.

As the months passed, the Catechism classes
proved to be really successful. More than that. A
few people began to follow a practice that made
me very happy. Every evening, in good weather or
in bad, they came to church for parish night prayers.
True, most of them were older men and women—
the young folks not yet being touched by grace to

I WOULD START A CLASS IN CATECHISM.

adopt this practice—but even so, it was a beginning.

"If I did a little more penance, it would help," I thought. "Something even harder than the fasting."

And what is even harder than fasting? Well I knew. It is to cut down or to interrupt one's sleep at night, and to use the time thus saved for prayer. This sacrifice, I told myself, would surely win extra graces for my parish. At least one or two young people suddenly would see worldly pleasures in their true light, would turn away from them in disgust, and would begin to find their joy in the things of God.

"It would be worth *any* suffering to have this happen!" I decided.

So I began to cut down on sleep. Yet when my first year in Ars came to an end, I realized that the price for making a parish really holy is very high. It is not to be paid easily or quickly. And what a mistake for the priest who attempts it to rely even for an instant upon his own powers! Rather, he ought constantly to recall his own nothingness as well as the nothingness of those for whom he prays. He ought to show this nothingness to the Heavenly Father, then beg—through the merits of Jesus Christ—that this nothingness be filled. And with what? Why, with the holiness of the Heavenly Father Himself!

"A saint is nothing but a person emptied of worldliness and filled with God," I told myself. "But oh, what a long time it takes for most people even to *want* to become emptied of themselves!"

So the days passed, and my heart rejoiced as I saw my prayers and labors beginning to bear a little fruit. Indeed, the Corpus Christi celebration in Ars for the year 1819 was the most beautiful that I had ever seen. All the children were dressed in white, and there was some fine singing. The entire village assisted at High Mass, though not many of the men would walk in the procession. That was all right for children, they said. As for them, they would feel too conspicuous following the priest about the churchyard with a lighted candle in their hand. It would be as if they were advertising their piety to the world. And of course it had never been the thing in Ars for any man to be thought pious.

However, there was one old soul who was not ashamed to walk in the procession. This was white-headed, white-bearded Louis Chaffangeon, who had attracted my attention many months before by his habit of frequently dropping into the village church for a visit to the Blessed Sacrament.

"I do believe that this is a really holy soul," I told myself, observing how the old fellow always knelt motionless in the back of the church, his eyes fixed unwaveringly upon the Tabernacle. Then one day my curiosity got the better of me.

"Well, good friend, and what is it you say to Our Lord on these long visits of yours?" I asked.

With a slow smile the old man looked up at me, his eyes as clear and confident as those of a little child. "Why, I don't say anything, Father."

"*You don't say anything?*"

"No. I just look at the good God, and He looks at me."

I could hardly believe my ears. What a beautiful

reply to my question! Only a soul that had given
itself humbly and completely to God could have
made it.

"If there could be just a few more men and women
like you, Louis!" I thought longingly.

CHAPTER NINE

IN APRIL, 1820, when I had been in Ars slightly more than two years, the Vicar General decided to send me elsewhere. He believed that I would have better health if I lived in the pleasant village of Salles. But as I reflected upon this, I felt sure that there was also another reason for the appointment.

"I haven't been really successful here," I told myself sadly. "More than half the people still stay away from Sunday Mass. And how many drunkards there are! How much cursing and swearing! Oh, surely the Vicar General knows all this, and so is sending some other priest to bring Ars back to God?"

It was with real regret that I made preparations for my departure. Of course I had never been liked by the tavern-keepers of Ars, and there were few farmers who would miss me. (I had preached too long and too frequently against their working in the fields on Sundays for them to be sorry that I was going away.) Yet I did have many loyal friends in the parish. Mademoiselle Marie Anne des Garets, for instance, and her brother, the Viscount Francis. And Anthony Mandy, Michael Cinier, Madame Renard, the Chaffangeon, Lassagne and Verchère families...

"Well, God's Will, not mine be done," I said, and paid little attention when Anthony Mandy told me that, in his capacity as Mayor of Ars, he was going to take a deputation to Lyons for the purpose of persuading the Vicar General to let me stay where I was.

I left Ars one morning in mid-April, together with my books and furniture. As the cart jolted us along the rough country road, I prayed very hard that I might do much better work in Salles than I had ever done in Ars. Silently I told the Heavenly Father that I would be willing to suffer all my life if only I might convert sinners. Yes, I would bear the sharpest pains which He might choose to lay upon me, and for as long as a hundred years, if only He would let me bring Him souls.

The hours passed, and presently we arrived at the Saône River. There we discovered a really distressing situation. Because of recent heavy rains, the river was in full flood and ferry service completely discontinued.

"But I've got to get to Salles!" I told the ferryman anxiously. "They're expecting me at the rectory. Couldn't you make a special effort to get across?"

Naturally the ferryman did not want to risk his small boat in the treacherous current. Seeing that I was a priest, however, and expected in Salles, he agreed to make the trip. So my furniture and books were loaded onto the boat and in a little while we got under way. But after two separate attempts to make a crossing, I could see that it was an impossible venture. Why, in that raging flood our little boat was nothing but a piece of matchwood! The ferryman had all he could do to keep it afloat, much less steer it safely to the other side.

"I guess I can't make it, Father!" he told me finally, breathing heavily. "You'd better come back in a couple of days when the current won't be so strong."

I thanked the good ferryman, paid him for his efforts, then looked about hopelessly. What was I to do now? What *could* I do? Nothing, I decided, save return to Ars for the night. So in a little while, with my furniture and books stacked behind me, I was back in the jolting cart and headed for my former parish.

"People in Ars will certainly be surprised to see me so soon again," I told myself. "No one there ever thought about the river's being flooded."

But if the people of Ars were due for a surprise, so was I. A short distance from the rectory I glimpsed a familiar little group standing about in earnest discussion. It was Anthony Mandy and his deputation, apparently just returned from the visit to the Vicar General. Then even as I looked, my heart gave a great leap. Anthony had seen me and now was running forward, waving some kind of a document in joyful abandon.

"You don't have to go away, Father!" he was shouting. "It says so here!"

In just a few minutes the whole story was out. At the office of the Vicar General my good friends had pleaded so earnestly that I be left with them that finally their request had been granted. The paper Anthony was waving so triumphantly was the cancellation of my appointment to Salles.

"Isn't it wonderful, Father?" cried Michael Cinier, the village councillor. "Why, it's almost like a miracle!"

I nodded, too overcome for words. Oh, how good God was! And this little group of friends! I must let slip no opportunity to repay their love and confidence.

As time passed, I did work very hard for God and the souls He had placed in Ars. Improvements were made in and about the church, including the building of a little side chapel dedicated to the Blessed Mother, the construction of a new bell tower, the restoration of the church ceiling and the building of a chapel in honor of Saint John the Baptist. The expense of all this was borne in large measure by the Viscount Francis des Garets, the generous younger brother of Mademoiselle Marie Anne. The Viscount lived in Paris, but he loved Ars and frequently came here for a visit.

"Nothing is too good for God's service," he told me more than once. "Father, go to Lyons and buy the most beautiful things that our little church needs. I'll be only too glad to pay the bill."

While I planned for the enlargement and decoration of the church, though, I did not forget another important work. This was with the children. Of course the Catechism classes were held regularly, yet what was a mere half hour a day for training little ones to love God and to be useful to themselves and to others?

"What we need here in Ars is a good school," I told myself, "particularly for girls. I wonder if it wouldn't be possible. . ."

Finally I made up my mind. Yes, it would be possible to have a good school for girls in Ars. As for teachers, what about Catherine Lassagne and Benedicta Lardet? Of course they were but young girls themselves, and they had had very little formal education. Yet they had piety, common sense and a willingness to serve. What was more, they loved children.

"Catherine and Benedicta will do very well as teachers," I decided. "But they'll do even better if they have some special training at the Sisters' convent in Fareins."

My two young friends were surprised and not a little uneasy when I outlined my plan. I would pay their tuition for six months with the Sisters of Saint Joseph in Fareins. In return, they would help me to teach the little girls of Ars about God. They would also instruct them in such useful things as sewing, cooking and spinning, so that when they were older they would be able to earn a living.

At first Catherine was a little doubtful about the whole affair. "Where will the school be, Father?"

"HOW CAN WE CARE FOR SO MANY CHILDREN?"

she asked. "And how much will it cost a child to go there?"

I smiled. "The school will be close to the church, Catherine, in a house that I'm going to buy. And it won't cost any child a thing to go there."

Benedicta could hardly believe her ears. "How can that be, Father? Surely it must take a great deal of money to run a school?"

I agreed. But we must not worry about money, I said. When, through love, we would give ourselves to serving God in the persons of the little children of Ars, He would look after all our needs. He would see that we lacked nothing that was necessary.

"And for that reason we'll call our school 'Providence,'" I concluded.

Early in the year 1823 Catherine and Benedicta went off to Fareins for their training period with the Sisters. Soon after, I purchased a two-story house, using the money my father had left me upon his death four years previous. Then I set myself to raising additional funds to furnish the place.

But alas for all hopes and dreams! During the five years in which I had served as parish priest of Ars, I had made many friends but also many enemies. Now the evil tongues of the latter began to wag with real malice. It was bad enough that I had done my best to close the taverns, they said, to keep the farmers from working on Sundays and the young people from their dances. But lately I had gone too far. I, who knew nothing of literature or history or the arts, was going to open a school! And supposedly a free one at that!

"You are both sly and conceited, Father Vianney," said one anonymous letter. "This new school is only a scheme to put money in your own pocket."

"You were asked to leave the Major Seminary because you couldn't learn Latin," stated a second letter. "Now you dare to think of starting a school!"

"Such an ignorant priest as you has no business hearing Confessions," declared a third communication. "The Bishop ought to forbid it."

These letters, as well as the slanderous gossip that buzzed on all sides, naturally caused me the keenest suffering. Why did certain people tell lies about me and try to spoil my work? I asked desperately. Above all, why did they accuse me of having committed the most dreadful sins?

"I guess I mustn't think anymore about starting a school," I decided. "Very soon the people will drive me from Ars with sticks and stones. Perhaps even worse. Because of the lies and gossip, I'll be forbidden to offer Mass or to administer the Sacraments. Oh, how terrible!"

There was good reason to worry, for just recently Ars had been withdrawn from the Archdiocese of Lyons and made a part of the Diocese of Belley. As a result, I now had a new superior and one who did not know me—Bishop Devie. What must he be thinking of all the letters and complaints that were reaching him? Then almost without my making any conscious effort to solve my problems, the solution presented itself to my mind with great vividness:

To fly from a cross is to be crushed beneath its weight, but to suffer lovingly is to suffer no longer.

I must start to pray for a love of crosses. Truly, all my misery has come from not loving them.

In the beginning it was hard to pray for a love of crosses, but only in the beginning. Suddenly, almost miraculously, it became very easy. And as this change took place, a great peace came into my heart. Trials which hitherto had caused me intense anxiety—the gossip, the slander, the anonymous letters—now only brought me an indescribable happiness. Oh, I thought, if I could just make everyone understand what a good and wise thing it is to pray for a love of crosses!

Yet I could smile at such a hope, too, for who would listen to me? Only a few pious souls. To the rest it would be meaningless, since from childhood they had been taught to fear suffering.

"Well, I can pray for a change in their hearts," I decided. "And who knows? Perhaps someday there'll be a miracle in Ars. Men and women, even boys and girls, will find themselves asking God for one of His greatest blessings: a love of crosses."

As the weeks passed, I gradually became aware of something truly consoling. *The more I prayed for a love of crosses, the less I suffered!* When, for example, Bishop Devie sent the parish priest of Trévoux to inquire into my character and reputation, I was fully prepared for a really great cross. The latter would hear new and dreadful stories about me, I told myself. These he would report to the Bishop, who then would order me to leave Ars and retire to some religious house to do penance for my sins. Never again would I be entrusted with the care of souls.

Instead of this, what did happen? Why, the parish priest of Trévoux sent a most reassuring report to the Bishop.

"Father John Marie Vianney is a good man, Your Lordship," he declared. "All the unpleasant things that you've heard about him are quite untrue. In fact, he's doing very good work as parish priest of Ars."

There could be only one result of such a report. The Bishop sent me his blessing, whereupon the lies and slander died away to almost nothing. And in November, 1824, as I had hoped and planned, *Providence* opened its doors to the little girls of Ars. In fact, because it was a free school, there were pupils from other villages, too, some of whom eventually became boarders.

"Sixteen children to care for and educate!" Catherine Lassagne exclaimed one day, a trifle impatiently. "Oh, Father! Surely we've undertaken too big a work for such a small house?"

I was silent for a moment. My young helper was a good girl, prayerful and hard-working, but by no means possessed of the blind trust in God which was absolutely necessary for such a project as *Providence.*

"How many rooms do we have?" I asked casually, ignoring both the complaint and the question.

Catherine hesitated. Surely I knew how many rooms there were in the house which I had bought with my own money?

"Why there's the big classroom on the ground floor, Father. Then two smaller rooms upstairs. . ."

"Three rooms altogether?"

"Yes, Father."

"And sixteen children live here, with you and Benedicta Lardet and Jane Chanay to look after them?"

"Yes, Father."

I could not help smiling, "Catherine, have you forgotten that the name of our school is *Providence?* Why, someday there may be sixty children here!"

Catherine's eyes widened. "*Sixty* children, Father? To feed and clothe and educate—*without funds?*"

I nodded. "Yes. And provided that we place ourselves and our work completely in God's hands, all will turn out well. But of course there must be no complaints or doubts. Otherwise *Providence* would be poorly named."

For a moment my young friend was silent. Then she looked up at me tearfully. "Oh, Father, I'm so sorry!" she murmured. "I'll do my best never to complain or doubt again. Truly I will!"

That same night an unpleasant though now familiar trial came to me. Scarcely had I gone to bed, utterly worn out by the day's labors in church and school, than I heard a soft pattering across the floor. A moment later there was a tugging at the bed curtains, followed by a series of harsh, gnawing sounds.

"It's the rat again," I thought. "And just as I was hoping to get a little sleep!"

Quickly I arose, found the light and looked about the room. But as had always happened before, I could find no trace of the rat. Nor was there the slightest sign of his having gnawed the bed curtains. Indeed,

everything was quite in order, and so finally I put
out the light and with a deep sigh returned to bed.
But I had scarcely settled myself for sleep when
the tugging at the bed curtains began again, followed
by the gnawing. Only this time both were far more
disturbing than before.

Suddenly real impatience filled my soul. "Tomorrow
row night I'll have a pitchfork handy," I determined.
"This nuisance, whatever it is, simply has to stop.
Why, I haven't been able to sleep properly for
weeks!"

CHAPTER TEN

The Nightly Visitor

ALAS! The pitchfork proved to be of no use whatsoever, for the next night the rat scratched and gnawed as usual without my even being able to see him, much less kill him. Then presently I forgot about the rat as far more annoying sounds came to plague me—heavy walking on the stairs, rattling at the windows, banging on the doors.

"Robbers are trying to break in here," I decided. "They want the beautiful new vestments that the Viscount Francis gave me."

This thought bothered me so much that finally I asked Andrew Verchère, one of the huskiest young men in the parish, to come and stay with me at night.

"Willingly, Father," replied Andrew. "I'll bring my gun, too."

My young friend arrived at the rectory at the hour agreed upon, loaded gun in hand. For a while we

sat talking by the fire, then at ten o'clock I decided
we should put out the light and go to bed. Andrew
could have my room, and I would take the one next
to it.

Poor Andrew! He could not seem to relax in my
bed, and at one o'clock he was still awake. Then
suddenly there was a violent shaking of the handle
and lock of the front door. At the same time heavy
blows were struck, as if with a club, against the same
door, while within the rectory itself there was a ter-
rific din, like the rumbling of several carts.

At once I sprang from my bed, lighted a lamp
and rushed into Andrew's room. The poor boy, trembling violently, was standing by the open window,
scarcely able to hold his gun.

"You heard the noise, my son?"

"Y-yes, Father."

"And you're afraid?"

"N-no, Father. But my legs...something's happened to them! They won't hold me up!"

I patted his shoulder reassuringly, then leaned out
of the window. "Well, there's certainly no one down
at the front door, Andrew. Perhaps at the back..."

But even as I spoke the earth gave a great lurch
and the two of us went staggering backwards. Clutching the lamp, I steadied myself against the wall and
tried to smile encouragingly at my young friend. But
Andrew's face had gone as pale as death. He no
longer even knew that he had a gun in his hands.

"It...it's an earthquake, Father!" he stammered,
eyes wide with terror.

I tried to be calm. "No, no, my boy. It's not an

"IT. . .IT'S AN EARTHQUAKE, FATHER!"

earthquake. And everything's going to be all right. Our guardian angels will see to that."

But as the minutes passed, I knew that I was just as frightened as Andrew. What could be happening to my poor little rectory? I asked myself. Why, the whole building was shaking and creaking as though some giant hand were trying to crush it to bits! And in the midst of all the commotion I could hear the same kind of splintering blows being struck on the front door which had aroused me from sleep in the first place.

"Merciful Father, protect us!" I whispered frantically. "Dear Blessed Mother, come to our aid!"

For nearly fifteen minutes the hubbub continued. The floor of my bedroom rose and fell as though it were the deck of a ship at sea. The walls creaked and groaned. Downstairs there were the thunderous blows on the front door, the rattling of the handle, the tugging at the lock. But then, and with startling suddenness, all was peace. The floor ceased its heaving. The noises in the walls died away. There was no more commotion at the front door. In short, everything about the rectory became as usual.

Quickly I pulled myself together and tried to assume a matter-of-fact voice. "Well, I guess you were right, Andrew. That *was* an earthquake, and quite a bad one."

For a long moment my young companion could only stare and tremble. Then slowly he began to recover himself.

"Father, if it was an earthquake, why isn't everyone in the village awake?"

I peered through the open window of my bed-room. Every house in Ars was dark!

"Of course it was an earthquake, Andrew. What else could have caused so much commotion?"

My young friend fingered his gun, hesitated, then swallowed hard. "Do you know what I think, Father?"

"What, my boy?"

"I think it was the Devil!"

I had to smile at such an explanation. Andrew certainly was wrought-up. "Maybe," I said soothingly. "But we can talk about all this later. Let's go to bed now and try to get some sleep."

For the rest of the night all was peaceful. No more poundings on the door, creaking in the walls, heaving of the floor. But when I asked Andrew to come and stay with me a second time, he shamefacedly refused.

"I think your rectory's haunted, Father," he muttered. "You'll have to get somebody else to stay with you."

After due thought, I finally decided to ask not one but two young men to stay with me at night—twenty-six-year-old Anthony Mandy, son of the Mayor, and twenty-four-year-old John Cotton, the gardener for Mademoiselle Marie Anne. They were husky youths with whom I should be safe enough.

The young men were more than eager to come. "You should have sent for us in the first place, Father," they said good-naturedly. "Didn't you know that Andrew Verchère is afraid of his own shadow?"

That evening, after parish night prayers, Anthony

and John came to the rectory. A group of older men armed with scythes and pitchforks stationed themselves in the church tower. If thieves were after the sacred vessels and costly vestments presented to me by the Viscount Francis, they said, never fear. They would descend upon the wretches without mercy.

Alas for such precautions! Around midnight there were the now familiar noises for my ears—the rumblings, the bangings, the knockings. But for Anthony and John and the watchers in the tower? Nothing!

"Once I think I did hear a noise," John admitted hesitantly. "It was like a knifeblade being struck very rapidly againt a water jug. But that wasn't anything to be afraid of, Father."

"No," I agreed. "You might even have dreamed that."

As for the armed men in the church tower, they had nothing more alarming to report than that lightning had flashed above the rectory in the form of a tongue of fire. But thieves and robbers? There had never been the slightest trace of these.

Twelve nights passed, and by now I was really frightened. The mysterious noises that continued to plague me but which no one else could hear—what was their meaning? Then, on a night when a heavy snowfall had blanketed Ars in spotless white, things came to a climax. Around midnight I was awakened by an unusual tumult in the front yard. It seemed as though an army were pitching camp there. Such shouting! Such confusion! Why, it was enough to waken the dead!

"But how strange!" I told myself. "I can't understand a word that these newcomers are saying."

My heart in my mouth, I crept downstairs. Surely Anthony and John must be aware of what was happening? My friends on guard in the church tower? Then why didn't they come to investigate?

At the front door I hesitated, breathing a short prayer for help. Then I turned the key, pushed back the bolt and threw open the door. But even as I did so, the blood froze in my veins. Why, there was no one in the front yard at all! The snowy surface was smooth and untrampled! And yet...and yet the tumult of a foreign army pitching camp there was as loud as ever...

In my great terror I could not utter a single sound. All I could do was to stare and tremble on the threshold like a man bereft of his senses. Yet after a while my mind did start to work.

"It's the Devil and his angels who are making all this commotion," I told myself fearfully. *"They're angry because I've been trying to convert my parish...now they want to frighten me so that I'll go away from Ars...above all, they want me to let the children alone...the very thought that these little ones are to be taught about God in our new school is more than they can stand."*

How long I reasoned thus, frantic and calm by turns, I do not know. But presently I noticed that the mysterious confusion had died away. More dead than alive I managed to shut the front door, climb the stairs and return to my own room. And as I did so, one thing became clear. In the future Anthony and John might just as well sleep at home. And the men in the tower, too. No power on earth could protect me from the Devil.

The Devil! At the mere idea of future visits from him I began to tremble anew. Of myself, what could I do against such a powerful enemy? Nothing! Absolutely nothing! He was a spirit, and could move with the speed of lightning! He could assume the most terrifying shapes! The greatest of all the angels before his fall, he still possessed extraordinary powers. There was not an intelligence anywhere in the world—even of the most brilliant man or woman—to equal his.

"Heavenly Father, only You can help me," I whispered. "Will You? Please? Because I'm so terribly afraid!"

As the weeks passed, it seemed that this little prayer was not to be heard. Each night as I made ready for bed I shook and trembled like a leaf. The Devil seemed to be everywhere. He knew that I was doing my best to save souls by prayer and penance, and he was determined to make me weaken.

"So you think you can live with less food and sleep than other men, do you?" he hissed in my ear. "Well, we'll see about that. We'll see. . ."

I groaned, knowing full well what was about to happen. As soon as I got into bed, the nerve-racking noises would begin. First, the Devil would patter about my room like a big dog, sniffing and whining. Or he might change himself into a cloud of bats and cluster upon the bed curtains close to my face. Again, he might make a noise like a herd of sheep in the room just overhead. Or hide himself in the chimney and squeak like a bird. Sometimes it seemed that in the room below he even turned himself into a giant horse, leaped to the ceiling, then dropped to the floor with an immense clatter of his iron shoes. Then again, he might move the furniture about. Or hammer nails into the floor. Or run over the bed like a swarm of rats. Or rap on the doors and windows. Apparently there was nothing that he would not do to interrupt my sleep so that I would be too tired the next day to work for souls.

"How am I going to stand all this?" I thought, shivering and shaking as I stormed Heaven for help. "Oh, dear Lord, where are You?"

Gradually, however, my terror faded as I realized that whenever the Devil bothered me more than usual, it was a sign that some great sinner would make his Confession to me the next day. Strengthened by this knowledge, I even dared to taunt my nightly visitor.

"How stupid you are!" I told him more than once. "Why, you think to frighten me, and yet you're always bringing the best possible news!"

The Devil did not like my making fun of him. In fact, his dreadful pride could not stand it, and often, after I had teased him, he would slink back to Hell and leave me in peace. Yet the next night he would be on hand again with more annoying tricks—growling like a bear, tapping on the water jug, buzzing like a swarm of bees, rolling my bed about the room, even attempting to throw me out of it by pulling away the mattress. At such times I would make the Sign of the Cross and give myself into God's keeping as best I could.

"A big sinner is coming tomorrow," I would whisper to myself comfortingly. "A big sinner is coming..."

CHAPTER ELEVEN

A NUMBER of sinners did come to kneel in the confessional at Ars, for God was now seeing fit to use me in a special manner. Yes, strange as it may seem, I who had not known enough after my Ordination to be able to hear Confessions was beginning to make a name as a director of souls. Every few weeks I was asked to help out with Confessions in the neighboring parishes of Trévoux, Saint Trivier, Montmerle, Saint Bernard, Limas. And with what result? Why, after my return home it was not unusual for one or more of my new penitents to journey to Ars to see me. Perhaps something was bothering them—a scruple, a doubt, a problem. Or they had brought some friend who had not been to the Sacraments in years. At any rate, the visits generally meant that I must spend quite a bit of extra time in the confessional.

"You're making our little church famous, Father," Catherine Lassagne told me one day, a touch of admiration in her voice. "There've never been so many people coming here for Confession before."

Benedicta Lardet, her friend and helper at *Providence,* nodded eagerly. "That's right. Oh, Father! You really are doing wonderful things for souls!"

Somehow the enthusiastic words of my two young friends toubled me, but I tried not to show it. "What wonderful things am I doing?" I asked slowly. "Tell me just one."

"Why, some days you hear Confessions for hours, Father."

"So do other priests."

"Yes, but lately people are having to stand in line to get to you."

"They stand in line in other parishes, too."

"Last week three really great sinners came to see you. Everyone knows that you converted them."

"Oh, no. I didn't convert them. God's grace did that."

"Well, there's a woman in Montmerle who says that you can read her heart like an open book every time she comes here for Confession."

"Ah, perhaps there isn't very much to read..."

Suddenly Catherine grew weary of the game I was making her play. "Oh, Father! You *know* God has given you a wonderful power to help souls! Surely you won't deny what happened in Trévoux when you gave the mission there?"

At this I had to laugh, loudly and heartily. For a truly amusing thing had happened at Trévoux. The crowds waiting to go to Confession had been so huge and impatient that they had nearly pushed over the confessional—and with me inside! Only after several minutes had I been able to restore order by stating that I would not leave for Ars until each one present had been to Confession.

"No, I won't deny what happened at Trévoux," I told the two girls. "In fact, I won't forget that mission as long as I live." Then in a more serious tone of voice: "There's a price to pay for all this success, though, and sometimes it seems almost too much for one poor priest. But if you and your little ones at *Providence* could help me..."

Then I pointed out to Catherine and Benedicta that—with the exception of the Holy Sacrifice of the Mass—there is no prayer which touches the Heart of God more effectively than the prayer of the young and innocent. Oh, if boys and girls could only know what power they have to do good for souls...to win the most wonderful graces for themselves and for others...

"You must have your friends at *Providence* pray for our parish every day," I declared, "especially for the sinners living here—the drunkards, the gamblers, those who offend God by sins of impurity. And if you can get the little ones to make sacrifices, too, how much easier it will be to convert Ars and turn it into a really holy place!"

Catherine and Benedicta listened in round-eyed wonder. Never had they realized how valuable children can be where the welfare of a parish is concerned.

"What prayers shall we have the little ones say, Father?" they asked.

For a moment I hesitated, realizing full well that the outward form of a prayer does not matter so much as the spirit with which it is said. "Have the children at *Providence* say just one Hail Mary each day for the conversion of our parish," I decided. "But be sure to have them say it slowly and fervently. Oh, what graces the Blessed Mother will give to all of us then!"

Catherine and Benedicta promised to carry out my wishes, and very soon I experienced the fruit of their efforts. Then as the weeks passed it became evident that still more sinners were receiving the grace to make a good Confession and to persevere in their resolutions to lead better lives. Thus, certain farmers no longer missed Mass on Sundays or dishonored the Lord's Day by unnecessary servile work, although for years they had committed both evils. Again, several young girls were now trying to find their happiness in the things of God instead of in dancing and other worldly pleasures. Finally, quite a few men had given up drinking and gambling in the four village taverns and elsewhere.

"The prayers and sacrifices of children do have a wonderful power to win graces for sinners," I told myself happily. "Oh, how wonderful!"

But even as I rejoiced, sadness filled my heart. Suddenly the Devil had planted a truly depressing thought within me—namely, that as pastor of Ars I was spending so much time and energy in converting others that my own salvation was in peril.

"Get out your holy books and see how many parish priests have been canonized," he whispered slyly. "Ah, what a surprise you'll have!"

At first I paid no attention to this suggestion. Then the thought came that it would do no harm to find out the names of those parish priests who had been raised to the altars of the Church and pray, humbly and fervently, that through their merits I also might do good work for souls.

Alas! A careful search of the Lives of the Saints revealed that numerous Popes, Bishops, monks, friars, hermits and even ignorant laymen had been canonized. But parish priests? Not one.

"What did I tell you?" taunted the Devil. "Ah, John Marie Vianney, how can you become really holy so long as you remain the parish priest of Ars?"

Gradually the disturbance grew in my soul, and I became almost convinced that it was the Holy Spirit who was warning me of the peril to my salvation which lay in my remaining a parish priest. How impossible it was to attain true holiness when there was so little time for prayer and meditation!

"If I could only be a monk!" I thought wistfully. "If I could just go off to some monastery and have peace and quiet..."

Yet even in my confusion of mind I put this thought resolutely aside. I had told the Heavenly Father of my desire to do His Will, and He had permitted me to become a parish priest in Ars. Until He should remove me, I should take it to be His Will that I remain as pastor in Ars, despite the multitude of distracting duties—that I should save as many souls as I could.

"Still, I wish I could have found just one parish priest who had been canonized," I told myself. "Oh, how much safer I'd feel then!"

But gradually I had relief in the evidence that God was blessing my priestly work in a truly wonderful way. In the fall of 1828, when *Providence* had been in existence for only four years, the enrollment stood at more than thirty pupils. The parish church had been enlarged and redecorated, with attendance at night prayers and membership in the various parish societies many times what they had been upon my arrival. Drinking, cursing, gambling and unnecessary work on Sundays also were beginning to lessen, with all the children and even several adults most faithful in attending Catechism classes. Yet the most outstanding change was in the great number of men and women, many from distant villages, who presented themselves regularly for Confession.

"Why do these good souls come all the way to Ars to receive the Sacrament of Penance?" I often asked myself. "Surely it would be far less trouble to go to their own pastors?"

Catherine Lassagne felt that she knew the answer. "It's because you're teaching them what you've taught me, Father," she said.

I looked up curiously, not quite understanding what Catherine meant. "Yes, and what's that?"

My young friend clasped her hands eagerly. "When you first came here I was leading a very ordinary life, Father. I wasn't committing any really serious sin, of course, but then again I wasn't. . .well, what I mean is. . ."

"Yes. Go on, Catherine. Don't be shy."

"I wasn't really *interested* in God, Father. In fact, I hardly ever thought about Him."

"And now?"

"Now I think about Him many, many times a day."

I smiled. "And why do you suppose this is?"

Catherine hesitated. Then, in a voice scarcely above a whisper: "Oh, Father! It's because you've taught me to love Him in a new and wonderful way. That's why!"

As I grasped the meaning of these words, my heart filled with a sudden rush of happiness. Oh, how good God was! He was using me, a mere creature, to bring other creatues to know and love Him! He was letting me experience one of the great joys of the priesthood—that of leading a soul to realize that God is all love, and that there is no earthly delight which can compare with learning to know Him and to do His Will.

Presently, when Catherine had gone her way, I poured out my heart in truly fervent petition. "Dear Lord, please help me to know and love You more and more," I begged. "Let me bring others to know and love You, too. Oh, if men and women and boys and girls could just understand how real You are. . .how close to them. . .how eager to make them truly happy. . ."

Suddenly I broke off. How impossible to put one's feelings into words when even the most beautiful of them could never describe the Perfection of God! And yet words had to be my tools, in the pulpit and in the confessional...

"Dear Lord, I'm willing to suffer anything if only You will bless my words!" I whispered. Then, after a moment's thought: "And if You could give me the wonderful grace to get people to... *to fall in love with You*...to stay away from sin not so much because it's ugly and deserving of punishment, but just because You can never be where it is..."

As I prayed, a mysterious new peace enveloped me. Somehow I knew that my petitions were being heard: that through God's mercy my future words in the confessional and in the pulpit would be even more blessed than they had been, and that I would be given the great grace of bringing many souls to an intense love of God.

"How wonderful!" I told myself. "How truly wonderful!"

And as I rejoiced, I thought upon the extraordinary power which love has over the human heart. When one person loves another, hardships and difficulties of all sorts vanish. Nothing matters save being with the loved one, serving him, making him happy. Confidence fills the soul, and the dreadful feeling of being alone and unwanted is as though it had never been. In a sense, one is reborn and possessed of a new dignity. But when, through grace, a person rises above earthly love to fall in love with God...when he gives himself unreservedly to His service...

"That is truly a foretaste of Heaven," I decided, "and a delight for every poor and lonely soul upon earth."

As the weeks passed, men and women continued to come in great numbers to make their Confessions to me in the church of Ars. And to each I gave the same advice: that, having received the Sacrament of Penance, they were to kneel for a few minutes before the Tabernacle and ask the Heavenly Father, through the merits of Jesus Christ, to give them a great love of Himself and of His Holy Will.

"The more frequently you offer little prayers like this, the easier it will be for you to become a saint," I said.

But while I did my best to win for these penitents the grace to fall in love with God, other matters also claimed my attention. Chief among these was *Providence,* the free school for girls which had no income save the donations of the faithful.

"Father, I'm afraid you'll have to charge at least a little something for admittance to *Providence,* or else arrange for most of the children to go away," Jane Chanay told me one day. "Why, we haven't sent any grain to the mill in months, so naturally the miller has no flour for us. And how am I to bake bread without flour?"

I smiled. Jane, a husky and somewhat headstrong girl from the country, was in charge of the kitchen at *Providence,* and it had always been a great trial to her that I refused to charge the pupils anything. Unlike Catherine and Benedicta, the two teachers, she insisted that depending upon the charity of others was a very risky business.

"You mean, we have absolutely no flour?" I asked mildly.

THERE WAS ONLY A LITTLE GRAIN LEFT.

Jane hesitated, then shook her head. "Well, not exactly, Father. There's enough for one or two bakings. But after that, what are we going to do? Because of the poor crops this year, there's not enough grain in the storeroom to bother sending to the mill. And other people are no better off than we."

An investigation proved that Jane was right. There were only a few handfuls of grain upon the floor of the storeroom.

"This is serious," I admitted. "But don't worry, child. Put all your trust in the good God, and go back to your kitchen in peace."

Yet after a few days I realized that the situation was fast becoming desperate. Because I had begged and borrowed so much grain and other supplies for *Providence,* no one in the village would give me any more. Rather, *could* give me—for there was a serious food shortage everywhere.

"I guess I'll just have to send some of the children away," I thought. "Oh, how dreadful!"

Then suddenly an idea struck me. Saint John Francis Regis! Suppose I asked him, and in a very special way, to help me? After all, in his own lifetime he had provided food for the poor on more than one occasion. Why couldn't he do the same now for the little ones of *Providence?*

"I'll take his relic and put it in the storeroom," I decided. "They I'll pray as I've never prayed before. Oh, surely something wonderful will happen?"

CHAPTER TWELVE

Miracles in Ars

THE children of *Providence*, not to mention Catherine, Benedicta and Jane, also joined in prayer to Saint John Francis Regis. Then one day Jane knocked at the door of the rectory. She had just used the last of the flour she had had in the kitchen. Now what was to be done?

"Go upstairs to the storeroom and bring down those few handfuls of grain that are left," I suggested. "Perhaps the miller could do something with them after all."

For a moment Jane looked at me as though I had lost my senses. How could the miller be expected to set all his machinery in motion just to make a mere cupful of flour? Yet stifling such doubts, my young friend went off to find a pan in which to put the grain. Later, when I heard her going up the stairs to the attic, I offered one more heartfelt prayer to him who had helped me so often in the past.

"Dear Saint John Francis, don't let me have to send any of the children away!" I begged. "Let there be grain for flour somehow. . .some way. . ."

Naturally it did not take long for the energetic Jane to reach the storeroom on the third floor of the rectory. But she was back again long before I expected—radiant and eager.

"Oh, Father! You just wanted to test my faith!" she burst out.

I looked up in amazement. "To test your faith? What do you mean, child?"

"But of course you knew about it all the time!"

"Knew about what?"

"Why, the wonderful new wheat! The storeroom is full of it. I could hardly open the door. Oh, Father, where did you get it?"

Now it was my turn to be surprised. What was Jane saying? Yet in just a little while I understood. Through the merits of Saint John Francis Regis, God had permitted a miracle to happen in Ars. In the rectory storeroom, directly above the place where I had hidden the saint's relic, there was now an immense pyramid of wheat. The top point reached almost to the rafters, the sides to the walls. In fact, so large was the pile that if one opened the storeroom door even just a little, grain spilled out into the hall and down the stairs.

"It's grain of the best quality, too," I murmured, scarcely able to believe my eyes, "and more than enough to provide us with flour for several months. Oh, how wonderful that now not one of the children need be sent away. . ."

Of course there was much rejoicing at *Providence* over the good news, especially among the orphans who had dreaded going off to strange homes. And unlike what so often happens when grown folk have their petitions granted, the little ones could not rest until they had said "thank you" to the friend who had helped them so wonderfully. What could be done to show Saint John Francis Regis how much his kindness was appreciated? they wanted to know. What special prayers could be offered? What sacrifices made?

"I think that the best way to say 'thank you' for the miracle would be to hear Mass in the good saint's honor," I decided. "That will give him more glory than anything else we can do."

So the Holy Sacrifice was offered in the parish church in honor of Saint John Francis, and everyone at *Providence* assisted with real devotion. But, strange as it may seem, soon the story was going about that it was not the good saint who had worked the recent wonder at all. It was I—the parish priest of Ars—Father John Marie Vianney!

"What a terrible thing to say!" I exclaimed when Catherine brought me the news. "Surely people will know better than to believe such a dreadful lie as that?"

My young friend shook her head doubtfully. "I'm afraid not, Father. You see, most of them insist that your prayers are so filled with faith and love that God almost *has* to grant whatever you ask of Him. Very soon I think there'll be more people than ever coming here to see you."

In one sense Catherine was right. From now on (it was the year 1829 and I was just forty-three years old) scores of strangers daily descended upon Ars. Many of these were good souls, eager to advance in the spiritual life, although of course there was also a fair sprinkling of idlers and scoffers among them. Then there was another group, too—the many invalids who somehow had been led to believe that I could cure them of this or that ailment.

"My little boy's been blind since birth," a woman would tell me tearfully. "If you'll just give him your blessing, I know that he'll be able to see."

Again: "My wife has a twisted foot, Father. I'll pay any price if you'll just fix it so that she walks like other people."

"My husband is dying of tuberculosis. I've brought him here to be cured."

"Here's my little girl. She's deaf and dumb. If you'll just put your hand on her. . ."

My heart went out to all these afflicted souls, but nevertheless I quickly assured each one that I could work no miracles. I was not a saint, only a parish priest. And a very imperfect one at that. But of course I would remember everyone at Mass and in my prayers. And of course I would do whatever I could for each man, woman and child who came to me in Confession.

Far from being discouraged at my words, the pilgrims continued to flock to Ars in even greater numbers. And as the years passed—1830 (a sad year for everyone at *Providence,* since it brought the death

I EXPLAINED THAT I COULD NOT WORK MIRACLES.

of Benedicta Lardet), 1832, 1834—really embarrassing stories began to circulate throughout the countryside. Yes, Father John Marie Vianney insisted that
he could not cure bodily ills, yet dozens of sick people seemed to feel better after talking with him.
Sometimes relief was immediate, at other times there
was nothing unusual to report until the pilgrim had
reached his own home. Then—why, sicknesses of
long standing disappeared as though they had never
been! And other favors, spiritual as well as temporal,
materialized with startling suddenness.

"The parish priest of Ars is a saint!" one person
told another excitedly. "He works miracles of every
sort."

"That's right. Why, just the other day the girl who
bakes for _Providence_ made ten loaves of bread from
flour that was barely enough for three."

"Yes, and don't forget the weight of those loaves—
twenty to twenty-two pounds each."

"You mean, Father Vianney was connected with
the wonder in some way?"

"_In some way?_ Didn't he pray that the dough
would increase as fast as the girl mixed it? Of course.
And that's not all. The good man has the most wonderful visions. The saints appear to him, the angels,
the Blessed Mother. . ."

"Yes, and the Devil, too. Why, I heard that the
Evil One actually grows so angry because of the
number of people who are coming to Confession
at Ars that he throws Father Vianney out of bed
every night!"

"No!"

"Yes. And what penances the poor priest offers in spite of everything! They do say that it's a marvel he can suffer so much for sinners and still live."

How my heart ached at such gossip! Certainly wonderful things were now happening in Ars, but not through any merit of mine. Rather, the Heavenly Father must be permitting the cures and other marvels because of the merits of the little ones at *Providence.*

"Try to explain this to people," I told Catherine and Marie Filliat. (The latter had come to take the place of our beloved Benedicta.) "Make them understand what wonderful power the prayers and sacrifices of children have with God. Tell them how our little orphans pray and suffer every day for all who come to Ars."

My young friends said that they would do so, but very soon they informed me that their efforts were having no real effect. Of course people admitted the value of the little ones' prayers and acts of self-denial, yet they still believed that I was the one responsible for the many blessings now being showered upon our village.

"But it's not so at all!" I cried. "Oh, if you could just realize how far from perfection I am . . . how irritated and impatient I become when certain people bother me. . ."

Yet even as the two girls stood there, silent and powerless to aid me in my trouble, suddenly there came a consoling thought. It was Saint John the Baptist (whose name I had taken in Confirmation) who was working the many wonders in and about Ars!

Oh, why hadn't I figured this out before! Several years ago a fine chapel had been dedicated to him in our little church. But had people prayed in it enough? Had they gone there with friends and neighbors to say the Rosary, to ask for help with this and that problem? Of course not. Therefore the good saint was now calling attention to himself by working miracles, although why he was permitting his namesake to receive all the credit would have to remain a mystery for the time being.

Quickly I explained matters to Catherine and Marie. "We must start to cultivate a real love for Saint John the Baptist," I declared. "Oh, how many extra blessings he'll bring to Ars then!"

Thus, in the days that followed, those who brought their troubles to me in the confessional were listened to patiently, absolved from their sins, then told to kneel for a little while before the shrine of Saint John.

"Talk to the good saint just as you've talked to me," I told each penitent earnestly. "Then see if he doesn't help you in a really remarkable way."

Alas! Although the pilgrims flocked obediently to the chapel of Saint John the Baptist in our parish church and numerous cures were wrought there and other favors bestowed, the rumor still persisted that it was really I who was responsible. As a result, I could hardly stir out of the rectory or church without being surrounded by crowds of admirers.

"Father, your prayers cured my husband of drinking!"

"We sold our farm for a good price, Father, just

as you promised!"

"I've been waiting to see you for three days. Could I have a few minutes now!"

"Make way, everybody. Here's a lame man who wants to get cured..."

"And a blind woman..."

"Father, will you bless this picture of yourself?"

"Here's a rosary..."

"Here's a medal..."

"Here's a crucifix..."

Little by little I grew quite desperate. How dreadfully easy for a man to give in to pride under such circumstances as these! "Dear Lord, don't let it happen!" I prayed. "You know that of myself I am nothing...that I have no powers except those which You have given to me. Oh, can't You let these people understand? Can't You make them see that if it weren't for Your grace I could easily be the greatest sinner among them?"

Then one wonderful day relief came. Suddenly, almost miraculously, I realized that it had never been God's Will that Saint John the Baptist or Saint Michael the Archangel or even Saint John Francis Regis should be my co-worker in Ars. Instead, from all eternity this mission had been reserved for a girl—and quite a young girl at that.

"Do you know who she is?" I asked Catherine and Marie and Jane.

The three shook their heads in bewilderment. "No, Father. Who is she? And where does she live?"

My heart singing with joy, I undid the wrappings of a small box. "Her name is Philomena, *Saint*

Philomena. And she lives here in Ars."

"*Here in Ars?*"

"Yes. She just arrived. Oh, my children, how you are going to love her!"

CHAPTER THIRTEEN

Philomena Makes Friends

ATURALLY, word concerning Saint Philomena's arrival spread like wildfire— that is, the arrival of her relic in the small box—and soon everyone was clamoring for details. Who was this new saint, anyway? And why was I so certain that now no other heavenly citizen was responsible when conversions and cures took place in Ars?

"Philomena is a little martyr who lived in the first century," I explained. "Not a great deal is known of her, save that she gave her life for the Faith when she was about fourteen years of age."

"Where did she die, Father?"

"In Rome. Her tomb was discovered there some thirty-three years ago, although it's just recently that the world is beginning to hear very much about her."

"And how did she die?"

"Probably by being shot through with arrows."

"You have a true relic?"

"Yes, indeed. It was given to me by Mademoiselle Pauline Jaricot."

"The lady from Lyons who founded the Society for the Propagation of the Faith?"

"That's right."

"She must have a great devotion to Saint Philomena."

"Oh, yes."

"Will you tell us why, Father?"

"Because Philomena cured her of a serious illness so quickly and completely that the Pope and his Cardinals were really amazed. Indeed, it was this cure which really brought about Philomena's canonization."

"And you, Father—you really believe that Saint Philomena is going to do great things in Ars?"

I smiled. "Believe it? My children, I *know* it!"

But much as I loved Philomena, I did not think it necessary to explain one of the reasons for my great confidence in her—namely, that several times God had allowed her to appear to me in all her heavenly beauty, and that recently we had made a wonderful agreement: that whenever a person came to Ars who wanted to be cured of a bodily ailment, I would send him to pray before the relic of my little helper. She, provided it was God's Will, would cure him. Most important, she would take all the credit for the cure and thus save me from embarrassing publicity.

"This should remain a secret between the two

of us," I decided. "It would only spoil everything if others should know."

As I had hoped, Philomena made countless friends in Ars, and by the year 1837 a fine new chapel had been dedicated to her in the village church. Some time previous I had secured a beautiful statue of the little saint, and now it was not unusual to see scores of pilgrims praying before it at any hour of the day or night. And close by her shrine the collection of crutches, canes, spectacles and other appliances, no longer needed by those whom the young martyr had cured, grew in size and variety.

Even as I rejoiced over these evidences of Philomena's intercession, however, I grew uneasy.

"Little saint, couldn't you work your wonders somewhere else than in Ars?" I asked one day. "If we're not careful, certain good souls will start to believe that I have a hand in them—just as they did before. Then I'll have absolutely no peace at all. As it is, I've seen people looking at these crutches and canes, then pointing toward me and whispering . . ."

In the beautifully simple way that saints have, Philomena spoke to me in the depths of my heart. "All right, Father," she said. "I'll ask God to let future cures occur someplace else."

My little helper was as good as her word. Hundreds and hundreds of people came to Ars, went to Confession, received Holy Communion, prayed at Philomena's shrine, then found their petitions granted after they had reached their homes or even on the journey homewards—but not at Ars. And such

PHILOMENA MADE MANY FRIENDS.

a variety of petitions! "To Philomena nothing is refused," became one of the most popular sayings of the day.

Yet as the years passed and my little saint's fame reached across Europe and even to the United States, I experienced a certain sadness. Philomena loved me, of course, but she refused to grant one favor which I had asked of her repeatedly. Even though I had now passed my fiftieth birthday, she would not persuade my superior, Bishop Devie of Belley, that it was time for me to retire from my parish duties.

One night in the year 1840 I grew really desperate. "I've simply got to go away!" I told myself. "The crowds, the confusion. . .oh, there's no peace for me in Ars anymore! I can't pray or read or think about God without being interrupted by someone. . ."

It was about two o'clock in the morning when I slipped out of the rectory. No one was about, and in the darkness I started down the highway leading to Villefranche without attracting anyone's attention. What matter that I had made no real plans? That I did not know whether to be a Trappist or Carthusian monk, or merely a hermit in some hidden spot?

"I'm free!" I told myself happily. "Free, after twenty-two years of being tied to a parish!"

But in just a little while various doubts began to assail me. Of course I owed obedience to the Bishop. And of course I felt quite sure that eventually he would give permission for me to resign as pastor of Ars. But had I dealt with the matter prudently? After all, running away from one's troubles usually means that one meets more and different ones, whereas if one faces the troubles squarely. . .

Then again, who would be looking after the crowds of pilgrims in Ars today? By running off like this I had not given the Bishop sufficient time to arrange for a successor. Perhaps right now—oh, dreadful thought!—someone was dying in my little village, and there was no priest to administer the Last Sacraments or to console the grieving family. . .

Gradually my steps grew slower. Then near Les Combes I glimpsed a wayside shrine surmounted by a rustic cross. For a moment I stood there, staring at the cross and meditating upon its meaning. Then suddenly I fell to my knees.

"My God, I've been putting my will before Yours!" I cried. "Forgive me! Help me to take up my work again. . .*Your* work. . .this very day!"

By dint of walking briskly I was back in Ars in just a little while, and I told no one of the morning's adventure. Rather, I decided never again to mention my great hunger for solitude. From now on I would use all my strength in trying to serve others rather than in foolish daydreams concerning my own comfort. For suddenly I had been given the grace to see beyond the barriers of flesh and blood to the priceless jewel which each person carries within himself—the immortal soul, made to God's image and likeness. What was more wonderful, I thought, than to give oneself to the total service of this jewel—in the rich, the poor, the young, the old—rescuing it when it fell into the slime of sin, washing it, polishing it, then returning it to its keeper all beautiful and shining?

"This is my work," I told myself, "and the work of every other priest in the world! Oh, dear Lord, what a really thrilling work it is!"

Soon I had settled down again to life in Ars, the desire to be a monk or hermit well hidden in my heart. And whenever this desire asserted itself, so that I became downcast at the burdens that were mine because I was a parish priest, I would find peace in remembering that each breath I drew was bringing me closer and closer to the fullness of joy.

"Heaven!" I would say to myself, relishing the very sound of the word. "I'm going to Heaven! I'm going to see God! The Blessed Mother! The angels and saints! And in just a few short years! Oh, what does anything else matter?"

Frequently I recommended such thoughts to those who came to me—the lonely, the discouraged, the sick.

"Listen to your heart beating, little one. Each beat is bringing you nearer to Paradise."

"My child, don't run away from the crosses God sends you. Transformed in the flames of love, they are like bundles of thorns thrown on the fire and reduced to ashes. The thorns may be hard, but the ashes are soft."

In His great mercy, God allowed such words of mine to comfort many souls. But as time passed, the strain of hearing a hundred or even two hundred Confessions a day caused my health to break. On the evening of May 3, 1843, just as I was beginning the parish May devotions, I was taken with a severe coughing spell and had to be helped from the sanctuary.

At once a murmur ran through the crowded church. Villagers and strangers craned their necks, then looked at one another anxiously. What had happened? What was wrong?

"Father's fainted!"

"No, he just choked on something."

"That's right. He'll be back in a minute."

But the minutes passed, and I did not return to the sanctuary. Indeed, I could not, for suddenly all the strength had gone out of my limbs.

"You've a bad case of pneumonia, Father," said the doctor when he finally arrived. "What's more, you seem to have had it for some days. Why haven't you been in bed?"

I made a gesture. "The work, Doctor. . . the pilgrims. . ."

"Nonsense. You could have had an assistant. Now you're going to have to stay in bed for several weeks. Even then it may not be so easy to pull you through."

I felt that perhaps the doctor was mistaken, and that I had nothing more than a bad cold. But on May 6, my fifty-seventh birthday, I was obliged to recognize my true condition. My heart had become badly weakened, and it was doubtful if I would ever be well again.

On the afternoon of May 11 the announcement was made that I was dying. At once it was as if some great calamity had struck Ars. The children, wide-eyed and fearful, left their games and hurried to church to pray for me. In field and home, tasks were abandoned as anxious men and women hastened to join the children. Every shrine in the church was ablaze with candles lighted for my recovery, and there was a constant coming and going, particularly in the chapel of Saint Philomena, where a pathetic chorus of prayers and sobs arose from the crowds kneeling before the relic of our little wonderworker.

"Saint Philomena, refuge of the unfortunate!

"Pray for us!

"Saint Philomena, health of the sick and infirm!

"Pray for us!

"Saint Philomena, new light of the Church Militant!

"Pray for us!"

And the pilgrims who had journeyed long distances to make their Confessions to me? Ah, these poor souls wandered about the church and the grounds like lost sheep, unwilling to avail themselves of the services of Father Lacôte, my substitute. Many had gone to considerable expense to make the trip to Ars. Others had only a little time to spare. What was to be done? they asked in disappointed voices. Was Father Vianney really dying?

"His four doctors say that he can't last the night," was the reply. "His pulse is very low."

"Surely Saint Philomena could cure him?"

"Of course."

"Then why doesn't she?"

"Well..."

Consumed with fever and barely able to breathe, I nevertheless knew what my good friends were saying and how much they wanted me to stay with them. For little by little those in Ars who had not liked me at first—certain of the young folk who believed that I was too strict about dancing, the farmers who wanted to work on Sundays, the tavern-keepers who had encouraged excessive drinking and gambling— all these had been led to another way of thinking and had exchanged their purely natural standards for supernatural ones. The result? Through prayer and penance our village gradually had become a really Christian community, and now I had not an enemy or an ill-wisher anywhere. Only the Devil continued to bother me. Since my illness, he and his wicked spirits frequently had gathered about my bed and tried to tempt me to despair.

"Ah, John Marie Vianney, we have him! We have him!" they had shrieked in horrid voices. "He is ours!"

On the night of May 11, however, my real agony began. The Last Sacraments having been administered, the doctor announced that I had only a little while to live. As the slow and mournful tones of the church bell gave forth the news, I summoned all my strength and consecrated myself to Saint Philomena and asked those who were watching at my bedside to see that a hundred Masses were offered in her honor and a large candle lighted at her shrine. Then I sank back feebly against the pillow.

"Another thirty or forty minutes," observed the doctor, feeling my pulse. "That's all."

Although I was still fully conscious, the power to speak or even to move was no longer mine.

"*My God!*" I thought, sudden terror clutching at my heart. "*Must I appear before You empty-handed?*"

Then like a frightened child I turned to Our Lady,

Queen of Angels, and to Saint Philomena. Oh, if
I might have just a little more time on earth to work
for souls! To prepare my own soul for a better
entrance into eternity!

CHAPTER FOURTEEN

A Would-be Hermit

A S I prayed, I felt new strength stirring in my limbs. Then to the amazement of the three watchers by my bedside—the doctor, Father Dubouis from Fareins and John Pertinand, the local schoolmaster—I opened my eyes. In a few seconds I had recovered my power of speech, and in a faint voice had resumed my prayers to the Blessed Mother and to Saint Philomena that I might be given a few more years of life.

About three hours later John Pertinand could contain his excitement no longer. It was now almost midnight, and I was still alive—*and still praying!* "What do you think?" he whispered eagerly to his companions. "Doesn't Father Vianney seem a bit stronger than he was?"

"He certainly looks stronger," observed Father Dubouis. "Ah, how wonderful if there's been a miracle in this little room!"

The doctor would not commit himself, however, for he knew the weakened condition of my heart. No matter how changed I appeared, how strong my voice grew in prayer, death could not be very far off. Perhaps two hours, four hours, six hours. No one could say. Then as I began to groan and toss as my temperature rose, he shook his head gravely. This was the end.

But it was not the end. At dawn, the dawn of May 12, I was still hanging on to life. Suddenly Father Dubouis announced that he was going over to the church to say the first of the hundred Masses which I had promised to have offered in honor of Saint Philomena.

"I think that Almighty God has had pity on us," he declared. "Father Vianney is going to get better."

A half hour later, just as Father Dubouis was finishing his Mass, God permitted Saint Philomena to appear to me with the message that my prayers had been heard. Several more years of life were to be mine, to be used in preparing my soul for eternity.

Overcome with joy, I stretched out my arms toward my little friend from Heaven. How beautiful she was! How kind! And how well we understood each other! "Oh, Philomena, thank you for what you've done!" I cried. "Thank you so much!"

Naturally there was great rejoicing over my miraculous recovery, and soon devotion to Saint Philomena was soaring to new heights. If the little saint could bring a dying man back from the brink of the grave, people told one another eagerly, surely she could work lesser wonders, too?

"Of course she can!" I declared over and over again. "Through God's mercy, Philomena can do anything!"

Eight days after my cure my happiness became truly complete when I was permitted to leave my room and to offer Mass in the village church. Of course I was still very weak and unable to fast for long. Hence, my Mass had to be offered around two o'clock in the morning. But even at this early hour the church was crowded, especially the little side chapel dedicated to the Blessed Virgin, in which I had chosen to offer the Holy Sacrifice.

I was forced to go through the ceremonies of the Mass leaning upon the arm of John Pertinand, but I was hardly conscious of my weakness. How wonderful to be with my people again! To see them gathered about me, silent and devout in this candle-lit darkness, their hands folded, their hearts and wills united with mine in offering sacrifice to the Heavenly Father! It was a scene that might well have taken place in the Catacombs, I reflected, and one which more than compensated for all the heartbreak and misunderstanding which I had known during my first years in Ars.

"Heavenly Father, bless this little flock!" I prayed earnestly. "And please help me to make good use of the extra time that You've given me. . ."

As spring gave place to summer, I offered these and similar prayers very often. And the thought was constantly in my mind that I had been spared from death for one reason only: to prepare for Heaven by serving God in some remote spot. Now that my strength had returned, the days for being a busy pastor were over. It was time that I left Ars.

"I think that I'll be a hermit for awhile," I decided. "Later I'll enter a monastery. Ah, what joy to be able to pray without interruption. . . to learn to know God better. . . to love Him. . . to serve Him. . ."

Very soon, though, I found that it was best to keep such thoughts to myself. My friends in Ars would not give admittance to the idea of my leaving them. Of course I ought to have a vacation, they said. In fact, I ought to go away at once for a rest of several weeks. But not to return? To bury myself in some solitude when I was so greatly needed by souls? Oh, no!

I paid little heed to their arguments, however, and early in September I secretly made arrangements for a visit to my brother Francis in Dardilly. This was quite in order, since weeks ago the Bishop had given permission for me to take a vacation whenever and wherever I chose. All he asked was that I should arrange for a substitute pastor during my absence. Well, Father Raymond from Savigneux was more than willing to take my place. He was a capable and clever priest some thirty-eight years of age whom I had known for a long time. In fact, I had been privileged to pay most of his expenses through the Seminary. Now he would repay me by taking over my duties as parish priest of Ars.

Yet as I completed arrangements for the trip to Dardilly, I was not quite at ease. Of course I wanted to go away. Of course I wanted to see my brother and his family, the old home, my friends and relations. But one thing was evident. I must plan to take advantage of this holiday from Ars in order to make a permanent break with the parish. After the visit with my brother in Dardilly I must go off somewhere and establish myself as a hermit. I must think no more of offering Mass in my beautiful little church, of hearing Confessions in the chapel of Saint John the Baptist, of praying before the shrine of Saint Philomena, of preaching to the people, of instructing the children in Catechism. . .

"It's good-bye to Ars forever," I told myself. *"Forever!"*

Then quite suddenly I knew that I could never go away without at least explaining matters to Catherine and Marie and Jane. Or without a few words to the children at *Providence.*

"It won't hurt to have a last visit with these good souls," I decided, "especially when I tell them that everything about my going must be kept a secret."

On the morning of September 11, I carried out my plan. I went over to *Providence,* visited awhile with the children, then informed Catherine and her helpers of my intention. Late that night, when everyone was fast asleep, I was going to slip away to Dardilly. And I would not be coming back.

For a moment the three girls looked at me in shocked silence. Then one by one they burst into tears.

"But you can't just go off and leave everything, Father!" cried Catherine. "What's going to become of the pilgrims? The children? The school? *Us?"*

"Father Raymond from Savigneux will be in charge," I said soothingly. "You know how clever he is, how full of zeal for souls. And since he's a much younger priest than I, and with good health..."

Marie choked back a sob. "But we don't want *him*, Father. We want *you!*"

Jane nodded miserably. "Yes, you brought us here," she muttered. "You understand about everything. There's no one who can take your place, Father ...really!"

I managed to smile encouragingly. "But don't you understand, little ones? God wants me to serve Him elsewhere. Now promise that you'll pray for me every day—and that you'll not breathe a word about anything to anyone."

Weeping with renewed sorrow, the three girls finally gave way to my determination. Yes, they would pray for me every day of their lives. They would assist at Mass for my intentions, they would recite the Rosary, they would perform various acts of self-denial. But oh, how hard it was going to be without me...how lonely...

"Ars won't be Ars anymore," said Catherine falteringly. "Oh, Father! Are you really sure that God wants you to leave us?"

I nodded slowly. "Yes, child. You see, since I was eleven years old my soul has actually ached for solitude. Now—oh, be glad with me that at last I'm about to find it!"

For the rest of the day I went about my duties as though nothing unusual were about to happen. Then in the evening I turned my footsteps toward the parish church for a farewell visit. And how my heart swelled with happiness as I went from one beloved shrine to another! Everything was so beautiful! The statues, the pictures, the gold and silver candlesticks, the tapestries, the altar linens, the many pious objects which I had gathered through the years to adorn God's dwelling place. . .

"Father Raymond should be very happy here," I told myself. "Oh, dear Lord, please bless his work for souls even more than You've blessed mine!"

Slowly the hours crept by. Around ten o'clock I went to my room, seemingly to retire. But I did not go to bed. Ah, no! When my few belongings were packed I began to go over my plans for still another time. Surely everything was in order—from the letter which I had written to the Bishop asking permission to lead a hermit's life in Montmerle, to the letter which I had sent to my brother Francis asking that he let me stay with him for a week or so in Dardilly?

"Of course everything's in order," I told myself comfortingly. "And in a few hours I'll be on my way."

A little before one o'clock I came out of the rectory and into the garden. It was very dark. In one hand I carried the package containing my few belongings, in the other my Breviary. But oh, how terrible! As I fumbled for the gap in the hedge which opened upon the church grounds, I heard people talking in hushed voices. Then here and there lanterns began to gleam.

Suddenly a man's voice rang out triumphantly.

"LOOK! FATHER VIANNEY'S COMING NOW!"

"Look! Father Vianney's coming now! He's over by the hedge!"

Stunned, I shrank back into the shadows and for a moment my mind refused to work. What had happened? What were at least fifty people doing in the church grounds in the middle of the night? Then gradually things became clear. *Catherine and the others!* Ah, yes. That was it. They had not been able to keep my secret. They had told some friend that I was going away. Then the friend had confided the news to someone else. . .

As I tried to collect my wits, an earnest little group of parishioners gathered close about me.

"Father, you mustn't go!"

"Oh, if you knew how much we need you, Father!"

"Yes. It's not right to leave us like this. . ."

"Please bless this rosary. . ."

"And this medal. . ."

Desperately I clutched my parcel and Breviary and began to push through the crowd. "My children, let me pass!" I begged. *"Please. . ."*

Somehow or other I did get through the crowd and down to the road. But as I recovered from this exertion my heart sank. I had left Ars behind, all right, but where was I now? It was so dark, and in my great haste I had strayed from the road and into an empty cornfield. Unless someone came along whom I could trust, the rest of the night would be spent in aimless wandering.

Suddenly a familiar voice echoed faintly through the darkness. "Father! Father Vianney! Where are you?"

I offered a quick prayer of thanksgiving. It was my good friend, the village schoolmaster! "Over this way," I called. "And hurry, John..."

CHAPTER FIFTEEN

The Lost Week

J OHN Pertinand had been teaching the small
boys of Ars for the past five years. He was a
fine young man, and since my illness had done
me many a kindness. But even so, I would not
listen to him now as he tried to coax me to return
with him to Ars.

"No," I said firmly. "I'm going home to Dardilly
for a visit with my brother and his family. Just show
me where the road is, and I'll be all right."

When John saw that my mind was really made
up, he gave a deep sigh and shrugged his shoulders.
Very well. He wouldn't argue any more. But on one
point he must be firm. I was not going to make
the seven-hour trip to Dardilly by myself. He would
accompany me.

I agreed to this readily enough, and more than
once as we trudged along through the darkness I

gave thanks to God that John had come. For because
of him there was now the chance to explain for still
another time just why I was leaving Ars. There was
also the chance to pray with a fellow human being.
Indeed, in between my eager descriptions of the
joys of serving God as a hermit and as a monk, the
two of us managed to offer ten Rosaries. But as we
came near Dardilly we gradually lapsed into
silence—exhausted from lack of food and sleep.

Of course, my brother Francis was beside himself
with joy when we finally arrived at his house. Ah,
what a long time since I had been in Dardilly! Since
he and I had seen each other! How much had happened through the years! How much there was to
say! But even as he welcomed my young companion
and me, Francis' eager expression changed to one
of grave concern.

"Why, the two of you are worn out!" he cried.
"And you, John Marie—ah, you're nothing but skin
and bones! And pale as death! Quick, we must get
you something to eat and drink. Then off to bed
with you!"

I protested feebly that I was quite all right, but
Francis would not listen. Or his good wife, either.
My room was ready and waiting, they said. And there
was a room for John Pertinand, too. Come, we must
go there at once. One of the children could bring
breakfast from the kitchen.

Gratefully I let myself be led away. Ah, how good
to be back in my boyhood home with its memories
of other days—of Father and Mother. . .of my oldest
sister, Catherine (who had died shortly after her mar-

riage)...of Francis and Gothon...of that other
brother Francis who had gone off to war some thirty
years ago, never to return...

"Dear Lord, thank You for the chance to be here,"
I whispered. "A little visit with my dear ones is just
what I need."

But the peace and quiet for which I had longed
so much did not last. Two days later the Mayor of
Ars arrived at Francis' door, desperately eager for
a few words with me. However, my brother refused
to allow any interview, even to admit that I was in
the house, and so the Mayor had to be content with
writing me a letter. After he had gone, Francis
brought it to me.

> "Father, don't decide anything yet," the
> good man urged me. "You are in need of
> rest; I know it better than anyone. Stay with
> your brother for as long a time as you think
> necessary, but don't forget your poor par-
> ish of Ars. Think of all those holy souls to
> whom you were showing the way to Heaven,
> and of all those who have forsaken that
> heavenly road and whom you will bring
> back to it..."

I was greatly touched by this letter, likewise by
one which arrived from Catherine Lassagne. But oh,
what bad news my young friend had to tell me! First,
my going away had nearly ruined the work of *Providence*. Already the enrollment at the school had
dropped from sixty to fifteen children. Second, no
one in Ars cared to work or to pray anymore. The

church was almost deserted. Third, Father Raymond, my substitute, was not at all liked.

"Come back, Father!" pleaded Catherine. "Things are in a terrible state here since you went away!"

There was another unhappy letter from a man who had opened a tavern in Ars, much against my wishes. Because I was no longer on hand, the pilgrims had stopped coming, he said. And how could he hope to have a paying business without pilgrims?

> "Father, I hasten to beseech you not to forsake us," he wrote. "You know what I have always told you, and now I repeat it with all my heart; if there is anything in my house that does not please you, I submit wholly to your will."

I was deeply moved by such sincerity, yet I was still convinced that my days for being a parish priest were over. God wanted me to be a hermit, of that I was sure, and so I tried to assure myself that the distressing state of affairs in Ars would be temporary. However, on the fourth day of my visit in Dardilly something truly embarrassing occurred. Early in the morning dozens of strangers began arriving in the village—on foot, in private carriages, on horseback, in carts drawn by oxen, by mules, by donkeys. *And they were all looking for me!*

"We want to go to Confession to Father Vianney," they told the parish priest of Dardilly. "Where is he, please?"

The good priest greeted the flurry of newcomers as best he could—fashionably dressed ladies from

Lyons, lawyers and doctors from Paris, businessmen from Ecully, university students, young married couples, children with their parents, even priests and nuns—but he steadfastly refused to disclose my whereabouts. He thoroughly understood and appreciated my desire to be let alone for a quiet visit with my family.

Very soon, however, the strangers had taken matters into their own hands and had discovered our house. Like an invading army, they descended upon the property and urged Francis to bring me out so that they might have my blessing.

My brother was quite annoyed with the pilgrims. "Father Vianney's a sick man," he declared. "He's not able to give anyone a blessing, much less hear Confessions."

"But sir, we've come such a long way!"

"Yes. I even closed my shop to make this trip!"

"So did I!"

"And I!"

"Look! I brought a little crippled boy with me. . ."

"And I brought this poor old blind lady. . ."

Francis shook his head grimly. "You might just as well go home," he said. "My brother is seeing no one."

From my room I could hear all that was going on, and suddenly I could bear it no longer. These poor people must not be sent away without the chance to go to Confession! Quickly I came outside, and to Francis' great concern announced that I would hear Confessions in the village church. But of course a messenger would have to be despatched

STRANGERS BEGAN ARRIVING IN DARDILLY.

to the Archbishop in Lyons for the necessary permission. I was allowed to hear Confessions only in the Diocese of Belley.

Francis was beside himself when, within a matter of hours, the permission was received and I was established in the confessional. What kind of a vacation was this? he wanted to know. Surely I was much too weak to be at everyone's beck and call? Yet it was only the beginning. The next day there were still more pilgrims, and even my sister-in-law began to complain. The yard was constantly full of strangers, she said. People were knocking at the door at all hours. They were even looking through the windows, so that there was no longer the least privacy for anyone in the family. As for meals—why, I was never on time for them anymore. How could I be, when the pilgrims kept me hour after hour in the confessional?

"It's not right, Father!" she cried. "These people don't realize how weak you are. . .how much you need your food and rest. Oh, why can't you send them away?"

I admitted that the pilgrims were an inconvenience, but hastened to explain that in a little while everything would be back to normal. After all, it was nearly a week since I had written to Bishop Devie, requesting permission to live as a hermit at Montmerle. Well, there would be an answer soon. And when permission did come, I would be on my way at once.

The next day there was a letter from the Bishop, brought to Dardilly by Father Raymond, my substitute. But alas! It did not contain the good news for which I had hoped and prayed. In plain words the Bishop declared that he would never allow me to leave the diocese, although he would permit me to become chaplain at Beaumont, a village some thirty miles distant from Dardilly. However, I was to weigh the matter well before deciding.

My heart sank as I read between the lines of the letter. "It's easy to see that His Lordship thinks I'm shirking my duty by going to be a hermit," I told myself sadly. "He really believes that I ought to come back to Ars..."

The thought weighed heavily upon me, and in the end I made an agreement with Father Raymond. The two of us would go secretly to Beaumont. I would offer Mass there and beg the Holy Spirit to enlighten my mind. And perhaps my young assistant would do the same?

That afternoon Father Raymond left Dardilly. Then early the next morning, without arousing the pilgrims' notice, I bade farewell to my boyhood home. Since it was very dark, Francis accompanied me as far as Albigny. This gave me the opportunity to apologize for all the trouble my recent visit had caused and to congratulate him upon his fine Christian home. What a good wife he had! What splendid children!

As the time drew near to say goodbye, however, my heart grew really heavy. Francis was fifty-nine years old, I was fifty-seven. It might well be, considering the uncertainty of the future, that this would be our last meeting upon earth.

"Oh, Francis!" I cried. "If you only knew what I'm going through! Please pray for me—*often!*"

Francis placed an understanding hand upon my shoulder. "I pray for you every day, John Marie," he said simply. Then, getting to his knees: "And now you'll give me your blessing?"

Slowly I spoke the age-old words which upon the lips of a priest have such enormous power to sanctify and to console: *"May the blessing of Almighty God—Father, Son and Holy Ghost—descend upon you and remain with you forever."*

Silently we embraced each other then and parted—Francis for home, I to locate Father Raymond, who had promised to wait for me at the church in Albigny, where we would each offer Mass before setting out for Beaumont.

It was a long, hard trip to Beaumont, and when we finally arrived I was quite weary. But I looked about with keen interest at the countryside—at the trees and lakes which dotted the landscape. How remote it all was! How peaceful! And there was real beauty in Our Lady's chapel which Bishop Devie was willing to give into my care. It was at some distance from the village, and tradition had it that Our Lady frequently listened to the prayers of sorrowing parents who came here on pilgrimage and brought back to consciousness small children who had died without Baptism, prolonging the life thus restored until the little ones had received the Sacrament.

"This would be a wonderful place to be a hermit," I murmured, gazing out upon the quiet woodland that surrounded Our Lady's sanctuary. "But of course, if it's not God's Will. . ."

Father Raymond looked at me curiously. What a change had come over me during the past few days! Ever since the Bishop's letter had arrived, I had been acting like another person.

"Well, what are you going to do, Father?" he asked presently.

I came to myself with a start. "I'll offer the Holy Sacrifice here as I planned," I told him. "Then I'll serve your Mass."

It was while I was serving Father Raymond's Mass that the Holy Spirit gave me to understand what I should do about the future. Certainly it would be fine to be a hermit here at Beaumont, to spend my days in peace and quiet. However, this was not what Heaven wanted of me. I had been given an attraction for the solitary life just so that I might sacrifice it in the interest of souls!

"Go back to Ars, John," said a little voice deep within me. *"Help people to love God, to turn away from their sins, to lead holy lives. . ."*

I bowed my head. For eight days—a lost week—I had been trying to do what I thought was God's Will. But it had not been God's Will at all. The flight from Ars, the desire to live in solitude, the struggle to be free of my heavy pastoral duties—all these were nothing but selfishness.

"Heavenly Father, forgive me!" I prayed. "I'll go back to Ars. And with Your help, I'll start to work for souls as never before!"

CHAPTER SIXTEEN

The Return

W HEN Father Raymond heard my decision, he made immediate arrangements for the return. A carriage was procured, and within a little while we were on our way. But how heavy my heart was as we jolted along through the desolate countryside of woods and swamps and lakes!

"I ran away from my people!" I kept telling myself. "Even from those who really needed me! Oh, suppose some of them died without being able to go to Confession? Suppose now that I'm not really wanted in Ars?"

As the hours passed, my heart grew heavier. The jolting of the carriage became almost unbearable, and when we reached Ambèrieux I told Father Raymond that I was not going to ride any farther.

"But we've more than four miles to go yet," he objected. "Do you think you can walk that far,

159

Father? After all, you're not very strong. . ."

"I'll be all right," I said. 'We'll find a stick some-where along the road, and I can lean on that if I get really tired."

So the carriage was dismissed, and Father Ray-mond and I set out on foot on the last lap of our journey. Despite my weakness we made good time, reaching Father Raymond's own parish at Savigneux, a mile or so from Ars, by mid-afternoon. Here the two of us entered the church for a little visit to the Blessed Sacrament. Then after a moment my com-panion leaned toward me. "I think I'd better send a messenger ahead to say that we're coming, Father," he whispered. "Do you mind?"

I managed a weak smile. "No," I said. "Do what-ever you think best."

After a few minutes' rest at the rectory, we started out again. And oh, how fervently I prayed that God would see fit to bless my priestly labors in Ars! Back in 1818, more than twenty-five years ago, I had gone there to work for souls. I had been young then, and inexperienced. Now I was fifty-seven years old and guilty, alas, of the dreadful fault of running away from my duties. It was no excuse that I had left Ars with the best intentions in the world, that I had really believed God was calling me to be a hermit. I should have been suspicious of the extreme cleverness of the Devil, who so often dis-guises himself and his ways under the appearance of good.

"Heavenly Father, don't let people turn away from me for what I've done!" I begged. "Let them trust me just as before, so that I can still help them to love You..."

Father Raymond and I plodded along, speaking rarely. It was now almost five o'clock, and purple shadows were beginning to lengthen over the fields. A faint chill was in the air, too, as the September day came to its close. Then suddenly I stopped in amazement. Down the road, the two bells in the church tower of Ars were beginning to ring—loudly and joyfully! And an eager group of men and women and children was hurrying toward us!

I reached for Father Raymond's arm. "My people!" I stammered unbelievingly. "My good people..."

Father Raymond nodded cheerfully. "Yes, Father. The messenger must have arrived with the news that you were on the way. See? There's a regular procession coming out to greet you."

My heart almost burst for joy. My loved ones held no grudge for the way that I had treated them! They were coming to meet me as children come to meet their father at the end of his day's work. Soon all would be as before. We would work and pray together. We would help one another to serve God faithfully. We would outwit the Devil and save souls...

In just a little while I was surrounded by old friends and neighbors, and to the triumphant pealing of the church bells we entered Ars.

"Oh, Father! Thank God you're back!"

"Don't ever leave us again, Father!"

"Please give us your blessing, Father!"

Leaning upon my companion's arm, happy tears glistening in my eyes, I gave my blessing repeatedly as I passed through the crowds in the square before the church. Oh, how good to be back! To feel myself so much loved!

"So all was lost?" I kept exclaiming. "Well, now all is found. I shall never leave you again, my children! Never again!"

After I had paid a short visit to *Providence* (where now only a dozen or so children remained), Catherine insisted that I should go to bed for a good rest. John Pertinand and my other friends added their urging, but I would not listen.

"No, let me go to church," I begged. "It's been so long since I was there."

So the hour of parish night prayers was advanced, and in a little while I was kneeling before the Tabernacle, ready to lead my people in the familiar litanies and devotions.

"Dear Lord, thank You for bringing me back," I whispered. "And please help me to make up for the lost week . . ."

The next day, I was surprised to find that there were only a few pilgrims remaining in Ars. According to Catherine, the majority had returned to their homes some days ago—convinced that I had entered a monastery and that there was not the slightest hope of ever being able to come to me in Confession.

"It'll be a different story now, though," my young friend declared confidently. "Why, as soon as word gets around that you're back, Father, Ars will be full to overflowing!"

Catherine was right. Within a week I was besieged with crowds of men and women who wanted to go to Confession. Some of these poor souls, alas, were deep in mortal sin. Others were in the state of grace, yet had made themselves miserable with doubts as to whether or not they were pleasing to God. Then there were those who had come not so much for Confession as to ask for health, success and other temporal favors at the shrine of Saint Philomena.

"Actually each of these pilgrims wants just one thing," I thought, gazing out at the vast throngs in the church, in the grounds, in the public square. "Peace of mind and heart! Oh, dear Lord! Won't You please let them find it here in Ars?"

In just a short time this little prayer was answered, and even more fully than in the past. Yes, Ars actually became the sanctuary of peace. And why? Because God renewed my startling powers to read men's hearts, and no troubled soul ever came to me for help without being comforted and strengthened.

Thus, within or without the confessional I could sense the dreadful stain of sin upon certain people's souls, even when these same people pretended to be leading good lives. To prove my knowledge, it was permitted that the past and the future should open up before me, and I would utter such amazing words of advice, of warning, of encouragement, that the sinners would no longer dare to conceal anything from me. Then, through the mercy of God, I would show them in what a detestable condition their souls were, and with just a few words excite in them a deep love for the Heavenly Father, a sor-

row for having offended Him and a desire to lead
a thoroughly Christian life. And of course I was also
able to comfort those who, for one reason or another,
believed themselves to be sinners and yet who really
were friends of God.

"How do you do these things, Father?" a young
priest asked me one day in an awed voice.

I smiled at my visitor, then explained as best I
could that *I* did not do these things at all. It was
God's grace working through me. I was merely the
instrument.

"I understand that," was the reply. "No one can
do anything for souls without the grace of God. But
still . . ."

"What, my son?"

"Why can't other priests work the wonders you
do in the confessional? After all, they're channels
of God's grace, too. And many of them pray very
fervently to do good work for souls."

I hesitated. Then I told my young visitor what
Father Balley, my saintly friend and teacher, had so
often told me: *The conversion of sinners begins with
prayer and ends with penance.*

"It isn't enough just to pray for one's penitents,"
I declared. "We must also be willing to suffer for
them—to fast, to go without sleep, to practice difficult mortifications. Ah, the pastor who doesn't pray
and suffer to make saints among his people is in
great danger of being a complete failure!"

My young friend was much impressed with these
words and promised never to forget them. Then he
told me of certain sinners in his parish for whom

"A PRIEST MUST BE WILLING TO SUFFER."

he had prayed very hard. In fact, for months he had argued and pleaded with them to come to Confession and there make their peace with God. But to no avail.

"Perhaps I've failed with these people because I didn't suffer for them as well as pray," he told me. "Do you think that's it, Father?"

My heart went out to the earnest young priest before me, and after a moment's reflection I nodded emphatically. "Yes," I said. "I'm sure that's it. And I'm sure of something else, too."

"What, Father?"

"If you can get the children in your parish to join you in praying for these poor sinners, in offering sacrifices for them, real wonders will take place. Ah, my friend, how many amazing stories I could tell you of what the little ones at *Providence* have accomplished through their prayers and sufferings!"

Prayer and suffering! Somehow it seemed that I could not impress the importance of these things too strongly upon the priests who came to me for advice concerning their work. God is so good, so merciful to the creatures whom He has made, I declared. And when these same creatures beg Him in prayer for a certain grace, then add suffering to the prayer—ah, what can He do but grant what is asked of Him?

Bishop Devie expressed considerable satisfaction with regard to the advice I was giving the priests of his diocese. But two years after I had made my attempt to be a hermit, he confessed his fears that the work with the pilgrims was becoming too much for me. I ought to have an assistant. And who would be better than Father Raymond from Savigneux? He was a clever priest, a good organizer, a splendid preacher, and, since he was just forty years old, his physical strength was at its height.

"You'd like to have Father Raymond for a helper, wouldn't you?" the Bishop asked me one day.

I smiled, "If you wish it, Your Lordship. He really could do much good here."

So presently Father Raymond left Savigneux and came to live with me in the rectory of Ars. However, in just a little while it was evident that the newcomer was making some unfortunate mistakes. Anxious that parish affairs should be better organized, he was attempting too many changes at once, and as a result he was unknowingly hurting the feelings of many good people.

"Why can't Father Raymond let well enough alone?" Catherine grumbled to me one day. "He was over at *Providence* all afternoon, complaining about the way we teach the children."

Marie Filliat nodded vigorously. "Yes, Father. It seems that he doesn't like our methods with the little ones."

"He told me that I'm wasteful in the kitchen and in the laundry," put in Jane Chanay tearfully. "And it's not true, Father. You know it's not!"

I hastened to comfort my three helpers. "Children, Father Raymond is a good man," I said soothingly. "And he means well. If he causes us to suffer sometimes. . .well, suppose we offer it up for sinners?"

At first Catherine and her friends protested that this was asking too much. Father Raymond was only a newcomer. If anyone was to give orders where parish affairs were concerned, surely it was I—not he. Yet finally the three relented. In the future, they said, if Father Raymond should criticize their work they would make a real effort not to become angry or resentful. And all this out of love for souls.

"Ah, that's fine!" I declared happily. "Such a sacrifice will win wonderful graces for some poor sinner. Just wait and see."

Despite all I could do, though, Father Raymond's zeal for arranging and rearranging parish affairs soon proved to be a great trial to many others besides Catherine, Marie and Jane. However, when two years had passed the difficulties arising from this cause lost much of their significance. For it was at this time that the Bishop sent the Rector of the Major Seminary, Canon Perrodin, to make known to me certain plans which were to make a heartbreaking change in our way of life.

"There's no use in beating about the bush, Father," the latter said, looking at me kindly. "His Lordship wants you to give up the work at *Providence*."

I stared. *"Give up the work at Providence?"*

"Yes, Father. You're sixty-one years old, you know, and not too strong. Certainly hearing Confessions all day long is more than enough labor for any priest your age."

For a moment I sat as one stunned. There must be a mistake, I told myself. Twenty-three years ago, and with my own money, I had purchased the plain two-story house that was *Providence*. To the last detail I had planned the work to be done within its walls. I had trained Catherine and Benedicta and Marie and Jane to help me. Now, to be told that I must retire. . .

I managed a little smile. "Canon, please tell His Lordship that my health is really very good these days. As for the work at *Providence*, it's never been a burden and never will be."

The Canon pressed my hand sympathetically. "I understand, Father. And I'll tell the Bishop what you say. But haven't you ever wondered what would happen to *Providence* if you should die?"

I hesitated. "Of course. But I've never worried about it. You see, I have three fine helpers— Catherine Lassagne, Marie Filliat and Jane Chanay. They would be perfectly able to carry on without me."

"And after their deaths?"

"Why, their own helpers would be in charge, I suppose."

To give extra weight to my words, I then launched into a description of the wonders which Catherine, Marie and Jane had performed at *Providence* over the years. The Canon listened attentively at first, then slowly shook his head.

"The young ladies may be all you say, Father," he admitted, "but I'm afraid that you'd better make other arrangements for them just the same."

"Other arrangements?"

"Yes. His Lordship believes that a community of religious—the Sisters of Saint Joseph, to be exact—

ought to come to Ars. He thinks that under them *Providence* would prosper as never before."

A dreadful numbness clutched my heart. Bishop Devie could never be so cruel as to insist that I give up my work at *Providence*. . .that I send away my three young helpers. . .that I let others, even the good Sisters of Saint Joseph, take over my beloved school and orphanage!

Or could he?

CHAPTER SEVENTEEN

Changes in Ars

WITHIN a few weeks, my worst fears were realized. The Bishop was in earnest about placing *Providence* on what he considered to be a secure foundation. In his opinion, as long as the teachers were laywomen, there was no guarantee that the undertaking would be permanent. What if, for instance, I should take it into my head to run off a second time to be a hermit or a monk? What would happen to *Providence* then?

Suddenly I realized that over the years I had allowed myself to become dangerously attached to my work with the little ones. Of course it was a good work, a wonderful work, yet was it more important than God's Will? Oh, no! And well I knew that for me God's Will would always be manifested through the will of my Bishop. I had absolutely no right to question any official decisions which he should make.

Yet even though I knew all this, it was not easy to be resigned to the new state of affairs. And how my heart went out to Catherine, Marie and Jane, who had worked with me so faithfully! All three were still comparatively young—forty-one, thirty-nine and forty-eight years old, respectively. What was to become of them now? I asked myself. They had no money of their own, since they had never taken a cent for their labors with the children, and apart from *Providence* they really had no home.

"Perhaps it could be arranged that they continue to live in their present quarters," I thought. "Surely the Bishop would give permission for that!"

The Bishop did give his permission, and on November 5, 1947, a contract was drawn up concerning the transfer of *Providence* from my authority to that of the Sisters of Saint Joseph. In this contract it was clearly stated that after the arrival of the Sisters, Catherine, Marie and Jane should have the right to live at the school for the rest of their days.

On November 5, 1848, the Sisters arrived. Catherine and the others, although they had had a whole year in which to prepare themselves for the great event, nevertheless found it hard to relinquish their authority. Everyone understood this, especially the Sisters, and before long it was agreed that the three should not live at *Providence* after all. Catherine and Marie would take rooms near the rectory and have charge of the vestments, church linen and the decoration of the altars. Jane would go to live in the village with one of her sisters.

On March 10, 1849, another group of religious

arrived in Ars. These were the Brothers of the Christian Family. They had come to relieve John Pertinand, who for eleven years had been teaching the small boys of the community.

"Father, your little village is becoming really important," observed various friends admiringly. "Just think! You'll soon have two fine schools here. Aren't you pleased?"

My eyes shone with happiness. "Oh, yes! God has been wonderfully good to me ever since I came here."

Yet as the weeks passed, I was afflicted with one doubt after another as to the kind of return I was making God for His goodness. Life! Why is it given to us? I kept asking myself. Why have we the ability to see, to hear, to speak, to go about from one place to another, if it is not to give glory to God and to help others to do the same?

"I'm not using all my powers," I decided. "Somehow I feel that I could do much more for souls, especially for those who aren't able to come to Ars, if I really tried."

Yet what *could* I do, tied down as I was to hearing Confessions all day long?

In the end it was Bishop Devie who gave me an idea. He suggested that, since I no longer needed to support the work of *Providence,* I might interest myself in the work of the diocesan missions. Several years ago he had helped to inaugurate a plan whereby every ten years a mission should be given in certain villages of his diocese. Since then the idea had proved highly practical and had produced much good.

"Of course it takes quite a bit of money to support and train the missionaries, Father," he told me. "Ah, how wonderful if you could help me to gather funds..."

I asked permission to pray and think about the suggestion for a little while. The Bishop willingly agreed, and so I began to call upon the Blessed Mother and Saint Philomena for enlightenment. Should I interest myself in the diocesan missions? Should I ask my friends to contribute to the Bishop's fund?

Within a few days the conviction grew strong within me that I should do just these things. Accordingly I took six thousand francs which had been given to me by various charitable people—about twelve hundred dollars—and sent it to Bishop Devie. It was not an exceptionally large sum, yet the income from it would defray the expenses of a mission to be held every ten years in two different parishes.

"The good that this money will do will continue long after my death," I told myself happily. "Oh, I must try to collect still more! Then other villages can have regular missions, too."

From now on (it was the year 1849) I gave myself whole-heartedly to the new work. I asked for donations for the missions from wealthy friends. From the poor, I asked for prayers. And when it happened that funds did not come in as quickly as I wished, I would take time from my work to go about the village peddling various items from the rectory. A chair, for instance. Or a rug. Or books. Even clothes which people had given to me, but which I did not really need.

"Father Vianney is turning into a miser," observed certain friends good-naturedly. "The first thing we know, he'll be selling himself for his missions."

When such comments reached my ears, I accepted them wholeheartedly. "Yes," I acknowledged, "I *am* becoming a miser—for God's sake. And if I could establish a new mission by selling myself, I gladly would do so. My one regret is that the inspiration for this beautiful work has come to me so late."

Eventually I succeeded in establishing dozens of missions. Bishop Devie was delighted and frequently sent me his blessing as a token of approval. Then on July 25, 1852, God called the good man to Himself. I was not shocked, for the Bishop was eight-six years old. And I did not grieve unduly, for surely there would be a great reward in Heaven for such a long and holy life.

On October 25 of that same year, however, I did have occasion to grieve. And to be deeply embarrassed as well. On that day Bishop Chalandon, Bishop Devie's successor, unexpectedly came to Ars and in an impressive ceremony made me a Canon of his cathedral in Belley. It was a reward, he said, for all my labors in the interest of souls.

"Canon Vianney, from now on you are one of my confidential advisers," he told me as I came to meet him at the front door of the church. Then, as the crowds of pilgrims gathered close about us, he placed upon my shoulders the mozetta, or cape of black silk edged in red and ermine which Canons are privileged to wear over their surplices. "Ah, if I could just tell the whole world about all the wonderful things that you have done here in Ars!"

Caught off guard (I had been hearing Confessions when Father Raymond had come to tell me of the Bishop's arrival), I was thoroughly confused and embarrassed. "But Your Lordship, I haven't done anything!" I stammered. "God. . .His grace. . .the prayers and sacrifices of my friends. . ."

The Bishop smiled and nodded. "Yes, yes. Of course. But there have been wonders, haven't there, Canon? And miracles without number?"

I lowered my eyes. "Saint Philomena, Your Lordship. . .the Blessed Mother. . ."

Suddenly the Bishop took my hand comfortingly in his. "Well, never mind explaining things now, Canon. Today is your day. Come—I'm going to say a few words to your good people."

Scarcely knowing what I did, I accompanied the Bishop and his attendants up the main aisle to the sanctuary. But even as we moved slowly along, I sensed the worst. The Bishop was going to speak about me from the pulpit! He was going to make the dreadful mistake of attributing to my prayers the many cures and other favors which had taken place in Ars over the years!

Then and there I made up my mind to one thing. I would take off the beautiful new mozetta at the first opportunity and never wear it again. I would sell it to some friend, and the money could go to the mission fund. That way I should be safe from pride.

Before nightfall I did succeed in selling the mozetta, and for the excellent sum of fifty francs—

BY NIGHTFALL I HAD SOLD THE MOZETTA.

about ten dollars. Then as best I could, I put the
day's proceedings out of my mind. *Canon* Vianney,
indeed! Why, what more thrilling title could any
priest desire than that which everyone naturally gave
to him—*Father?* From the day of my Ordination this
beautiful name had been like music in my ears, especially on the lips of little children.

"Love and trust and reverence are in this name,"
I told myself. "I never want to be called by any other."

The months passed, and I continued to busy
myself with collecting for the "ten-year mission
fund," and also in hearing Confessions. But in the
summer of 1853 the dreadful doubts of which I had
for some time been free began to rush in on me
once more. I had so little time to give to God in
private prayer! Apart from Mass and the Divine
Office, my whole day was spent in hearing Confessions, in comforting and advising and encouraging
the hundreds of souls who came to Ars to see me.

Finally I became almost desperate. I was sixty-
seven years old now, and surely my time on earth
was drawing to a close. Yet where was the chance
to call to mind my own sins, to weep over them,
to prepare myself for Heaven?

"If I could just go away to some quiet spot!" I
thought longingly. "If I could just be a hermit or
a monk and have the chance to pray. . .and *to*
think . . ."

One August day came the opportunity for which
I had been waiting. A letter arrived from the Marist
Fathers, saying that I might come to live in their
house of recollection at La Neylière. Since perpetual

silence was observed here, there would be no crowds of visitors. I would be free from all those pastoral duties which had weighed so heavily upon me for more than thirty-five years. In fact, I would be entering upon a life that was almost like that of a Trappist monk.

I could hardly restrain my joy. I had never seen the Marist house at La Neylière, but I had heard a great deal about it. It was in the country, some thirty miles from Lyons, and was surrounded by beautiful hills and woods. Of course it was not a large place, for it had just been opened the year before and as yet only a dozen priests and Brothers were established there. But from all accounts these twelve men were saints. To be permitted to live among them was indeed a privilege.

For a while I kept the good news to myself. Then on Thursday, the first day of September, when Catherine brought my dinner to my room, I decided to share my secret with her.

"Child, I'm going to join the Marists at La Neylière next week," I said simply. "Will you please pray that I shall serve God well there?"

For a moment Catherine looked at me in stunned silence. Then her face paled and she all but collapsed. "Father, you don't mean it!" she wailed. "You're not going to try to leave us again!"

I nodded cheerfully. "Yes. Everything's settled. The good Fathers have promised to give me a little room of my own. There will be perpetual Exposition of the Blessed Sacrament, absolute silence, regular hours for prayer and meditation..."

"But Father! Don't you remember what happened ten years ago when you tried to run away? The pilgrims followed you to Dardilly! They upset everything for your poor brother and his family..."

"Ah, but that was ten years ago, Catherine. I'm an old man now, and the pilgrims have had enough of me. They'll never try to follow me this time."

"But they will, Father! You know they will! Then there's Bishop Chalandon..."

"He'll let me go. I'll write him a letter today."

Suddenly Catherine stretched out both hands pleadingly. "Oh, Father, please don't do it! Please don't even think of it!"

I hesitated, then shook my head firmly. What was the use of talking anymore? My mind was made up. This was Thursday. On Monday, very early in the morning, I would go to Lyons, where my sister Gothon and her husband were living. After a short visit here, I would set out for La Neylière...and peace.

"Child, it's God's Will that I go," I said gently. "Come, promise that you'll not say a word of what I've told you to anyone?"

For a long moment Catherine looked at me—her face drawn, her eyes brimming with tears. Then choking back a sob, she nodded slowly. "I promise, Father. But oh, what a terrible mistake you're making!"

CHAPTER EIGHTEEN

HEAVEN seemed to favor all my plans. Within
a few hours after my talk with Catherine,
I learned that Ars was to have a new curate.
He was Father Toccanier, a thirty-one-year-old missionary from Pont-d'Ain. He would replace Father
Raymond, who was being transferred to another parish after eight years' residence in Ars. Even more,
Bishop Chalandon had announced that I might have
as many other assistants as I wished.

I gave a great sigh of relief. "If the Bishop has
that many priests to spare, I can go to La Neylière
with a really clear conscience," I told myself happily. "Oh, how splendid!"

On Saturday afternoon Father Toccanier arrived
in Ars, and on Sunday morning he officiated at the
Holy Mass in the village church. As I watched him
offer the Holy Sacrifice, my heart swelled with joy.

How devout he was! How filled with love of God! Why, his face was actually radiant as he sang the prayers from the Missal!

"Right now this young priest believes himself to be just my assistant," I thought, smiling. "Ah, but wait until tomorrow! What a surprise he'll have when he finds I've gone to La Neylière, and that he is really the parish priest of Ars!"

Sunday passed quietly. Toward evening I made a few simple preparations for my trip and also wrote a letter to Bishop Chalandon, explaining my decision and asking for his blessing on my new life. But at about eight o'clock my peace of mind was somewhat disturbed. Catherine came to me, her eyes red with weeping.

"You made me promise to keep everything a secret, Father," she faltered. "And so far I have. But you know that Marie Filliat worked at Providence, too. And she's going to be very hurt if you go off without a word. . .and angry with me as well. . ."

I hesitated. "I suppose you want to tell her everything?"

"Yes, Father. You see, she lives with me and it seems only fair. . ."

"Very well. You may tell her the news. But see that she keeps it a secret."

In just a little while Catherine was back, accompanied by Marie. The two were crying as though their hearts would break, but nothing they said could make me change my mind. I was going to live with the Marist Fathers at La Neylière, and that was that. Finally, to put an end to the distressing interview,

I gave Catherine the letter which I had written to the Bishop and made her promise to see that it was delivered promptly. Then I raised my hand in blessing.

"I'll be leaving around midnight," I said. "Good-bye, my children."

Suddenly a change came over Catherine and she became quite calm. "Father, you simply can't go alone to Lyons. You might have a fainting spell," she declared respectfully. "I think that the two of us had better go with you."

I stared in amazement. "What?"

Marie also was taken by surprise, but she brushed back her tears and nodded vigorously. "Yes, Father. We'll prepare some provisions—something nourishing to eat and drink. After all, a trip of twenty-five miles. . ."

"We'll take a lantern, too. You know how dark it is these nights. Why, you might easily stumble and fall."

"You might hurt yourself seriously and never even reach Lyons."

"Then what would happen to your plans for going to the Marists?"

I looked about helplessly. "I planned to go alone," I objected. "Everything was to be a secret. This way—"

"Ah, but this way is really a much better way, Father," put in Catherine soothingly. "We'll see that you get safely to your sister's house in Lyons. From there you can go to La Neylière whenever you wish."

In the end I gave in to Catherine and Marie. Very

well. The two might accompany me to Lyons. I would meet them outside the rectory shortly after midnight.

At the appointed hour I crept softly down the stairs and out into the darkness. As they had promised, Catherine and Marie were waiting with a basket of provisions and a lantern. But oh, how dreadful! By the flickering light of the lantern I could make out three other people who had no business whatever in being on hand—Brother Athanasius (the superior of the little religious community which taught the small boys of Ars), Brother Jerome, his assistant, and Father Toccanier, my newly-arrived curate.

Quickly I turned an accusing eye on Catherine. "You...you've sold me!" I burst out.

Startled by the bitterness in my voice, Catherine hid her face in her hands and began to cry. But as I turned to reproach Marie for likewise having broken her word, Brother Athanasius touched me on the arm.

"Father, you're not going to leave us," he said kindly. "There's been some kind of a mistake, hasn't there?"

I clutched my Breviary and umbrella in a firmer grip. "No," I muttered. "There's been no mistake. And I can't talk now, Brother. I'm in a hurry."

"But Father! If you really mean to go, we must let your friends know by ringing the church bell. Why, there must be five hundred pilgrims praying in the church right now. And all of them have come to Ars to see you, Father, to go to Confession..."

Brother Jerome nodded eagerly. "Yes, and when

we ring the bell, they'll all come running, Father. They'll insist on going with you. Why, I'll go along myself. And so will everyone else in Ars."

I turned away abruptly. "Follow me if you wish, but don't keep me now," I said, and hurried off. But it was very dark, and before long I realized that I was going in the wrong direction. To make matters worse, the pilgrims had sensed that something unusual was happening. Unable to concentrate on their prayers, they were now rushing out of the church in excited throngs—many with lighted candles in their hands.

"Wait, Father!" cried one man desperately. "I've simply got to talk with you!"

A woman was close behind him. "You promised to bless my little girl, Father!" she exclaimed. "Look! She's here with me now. . ."

By reason of the darkness and the unexpected rush of pilgrims, I was suddenly and thoroughly confused. Where was the little brook that I had to cross in order to reach the highway? There was a bridge of planks. . .

"This way, Father," called Brother Jerome, who somehow had possessed himself of Catherine's lantern. "Just follow me and you'll be all right."

Scarcely knowing what I did, I began to follow Brother Jerome—being followed in turn by Catherine, Marie and dozens of other friends. But as we reached the brook, Father Toccanier suddenly appeared and placed himself resolutely before me on the low plank bridge. "No, you mustn't go like this, Father," he declared. "It's not right."

I struggled to get by my young curate. "Let me pass!" I begged. *"Let me pass!"*

But Father Toccanier would not budge. Then, before I could make up my mind what to do, he seized the Breviary from under my arm and thrust it into Catherine's hands. "Go away and do not come back," he told her.

"M-my Breviary! Give it to me at once!" I stammered indignantly.

"Not until you promise to stay with us, Father."

"You . . .you have no right to take my Breviary!"

"You may have it back when you decide to come with us."

"In that case," I replied, "I must go without it and say my Office when I get to Lyons."

Marie Filliat looked at me in astonishment. *"Father!* You don't mean to say that you'd let the hours of the day go by without saying at least some of the Office!"

"Well. . ."

"Why, that would be giving bad example, Father! Terribly bad example!"

"I have another Breviary in my room," I said, after a moment's hesitation, "the one which Bishop Devie left to me when he died. . ."

Father Toccanier smiled, and took me gently by the arm. "Suppose we go and get it," he suggested. "It will take but a minute or two."

Feeling rather helpless, I let myself be persuaded. But we had gone less than a hundred feet toward the rectory when the church bell began to ring—slowly, solemnly—a signal to the countryside that

"GIVE ME MY BREVIARY!"

something unusual was happening. However, in my great agitation I believed Father Toccanier when he said that it was the Angelus (for in Ars it was the custom to ring it around one o'clock in the morning), and so I knelt for the accustomed prayers. Never did it occur to me that this was another way in which my new assistant was trying to delay my flight to Lyons as much as possible, and that he had sent for the Mayor and various influential people so that they might add their protests to his.

When the prayers of the Angelus were finished, I started to rise from my knees. But Father Toccanier stretched out a restraining hand. "Suppose we say a decade of the Rosary so that you may have a safe journey to Lyons, Father," he suggested. "You know that it's a long, hard trip."

Quite suddenly my suspicion was aroused. "No," I said hastily, "I can say my Rosary on the way."

Then, before Father Toccanier could utter another word, I was on my feet fairly running toward the rectory. In vain did several people place themselves in my path. In my room were eight large volumes of the Breviary, bound in dark green leather. My only concern was to get there at once, choose the correct volume, and then start out for Lyons.

Alas! Father Toccanier was thirty-six years younger than I, and far quicker on his feet. Despite my best efforts, he succeeded in reaching the rectory before me, and there changed the order of the volumes of the Breviary. Consequently, when I did arrive, I lost much valuable time in searching for the right book. Then, just as I found it, Father

Toccanier pointed to a picture of Bishop Devie which was hanging on the wall.

"Look, Father! See how Bishop Devie is frowning at you from Heaven!"

I paused, my hand on the green leather volume. The eyes of my dead superior *were* looking at me! And they *were* severe! Still, it was only a picture. . .

"Bishop Devie won't reproach me," I said. "He knows very well that I have need to go and weep for my poor life."

My assistant shook his head. "Father, the will of a Bishop must be respected during his lifetime, and even more when he is dead. Don't you remember what he told you ten years ago?"

Suddenly uncontrollable impatience seized me. "No! No!" I cried. "I've got to go!" And snatching the volume of the Breviary, I rushed from the room and down the stairs.

But what a scene now met my eyes! Aroused by the sound of the church bell (which some minutes before had changed from a mournful dirge to a vigorous clanging), all of Ars was on hand. Some cried out that there was a fire. Others insisted that robbers had broken into the church. Lanterns were everywhere, and scores of people were descending upon the village square armed with buckets, pitchforks, scythes and clubs. But as I tried to leave the rectory and lose myself in the hubbub, the village cobbler loomed suddenly in the doorway.

"No, Father. I have orders not to let you pass."

"But my son. . ."

"It's no use, Father. I gave my word."

I paid no attention, and tried to push the good man aside. But to no avail. He was too strong. However, when Father Toccanier suddenly appeared and made a sign, the cobbler allowed me to cross the threshold and to go a short distance into the yard.

For a moment I stood here surveying the tumultuous scene—the crowds, the flickering lanterns, the ever-increasing groups massing in the square with their buckets and scythes and clubs. Ah, surely if I watched my chance I could make my escape amidst so much confusion? Then suddenly a number of women pilgrims came hurrying out of the church directly toward me. Most of them were strangers to Ars, and nearly all of them were in tears.

"Don't go, Father!" cried one, falling at my feet. "I haven't been to Confession in twelve years!"

"I came all the way from Calais, Father!" sobbed another. "Surely you'll let me have five minutes of your time?"

"My boy! Give my boy your blessing, Father!"

"Here's my little girl, Father. She's been blind since birth!"

"You promised that I could see you today, Father. Don't you remember?"

"My husband, Father! He'll never talk to any priest but you!"

At once a wave of pity arose within me. My sisters, my brothers in Christ! How could I leave them like this? And yet if I did not leave, I would never have the chance to prepare my own soul for eternity. . .

"I. . .I've got to go," I muttered. "Oh, my

children...my children...*God bless you!*"

However, just as I tried to turn away, Father Toccanier gripped my arm firmly. "Father, have you forgotten Saint Martin? And Saint Philip Neri?"

I stared in amazement. "*Saint Martin? Saint Philip Neri?*"

"Yes. Don't you remember how Martin, old and tired, longed for death, but said that if God willed him to live on he would not 'refuse the labor'? And Philip, who said that were he to stand on the threshold of Paradise and a sinner called out to him, he would gladly leave the court of Heaven in order to hear his Confession?"

I hesitated, then nodded slowly. "Yes. I...I remember."

"And still you plan to leave us? You won't help these poor souls who have suffered so much to come to Ars?"

I bowed my head and for a moment was silent, praying and thinking, while on all sides the pilgrims redoubled their pleas that I remain with them. Then suddenly I lifted my eyes.

"Let us go over to the church," I said simply.

CHAPTER NINETEEN

The Work Continues

I PRAYED for a long while in the church, then went to the sacristy. Crowds of weeping pilgrims pressed about me, among whom was the Mayor of Ars. He was in the act of pleading with me to remain as pastor when, to his utter astonishment, I suddenly turned from him, seized my surplice and started toward the confessional. At once there was a great cry of joy, and the pilgrims surged forward and all but carried me.

"Father Vianney isn't going to leave us!" they exclaimed incredulously. "Oh, God be praised!"

I had indeed decided to stay in Ars. At that moment Heaven had shown me (and for the third time!) that my wish to lead a secluded life was a temptation of the Devil. I had been born to be a parish priest—no more, no less. And I would save my soul by doing *my* duty, not that of anyone else, no matter how holy or how necessary it might be. I would attain perfection by being a devoted pastor, by meeting people, advising and encouraging them, helping them to think frequently and fervently of God, absolving them from their sins if they should weaken and fall away from Him. In short, I would prepare myself for eternity simply by staying in Ars and doing each day's priestly work as well as I could.

As the weeks passed and the work for souls seemed at times beyond my strength, a little voice deep in my heart encouraged me to persevere:

"John, you're sixty-seven years old, but you're really just beginning to learn some important things about holiness."

I listened carefully. "What things?"

"Two things—that time given to helping a neighbor need never be taken from God, and that time given to God need never be taken from a neighbor."

Suddenly it was as though a light had been turned on within me. God and neighbor! In one sense they were the same. It was impossible to love one deeply and sincerely without loving the other. Oh, what a dreadful pity that individuals and nations were not guided by these truths! For they were like birds struggling to fly with only one wing. Try though they would, they could never reach the heights.

"I must use both wings," I thought, "love of neighbor as well as love of God. And I must help all those who will come to me to do the same. . ."

All those who would come to me! By the year 1855 (two years after my third attempt to leave Ars) the pilgrims numbered several thousand each month.

When my brother Francis died, on April 6 of that year, I prayed with all my strength that he would secure for me the grace to help as many of these as I could. And since I was a member of the Third Order of Mary and of the Third Order of Saint Francis, I also prayed to my fellow tertiaries in Heaven for the same grace.

Presently there was great excitement in Ars. On August 15 the newspapers announced that the Emperor was bestowing an important honor upon certain men who had rendered distinguished service to the French nation. He was making each a Knight of the Imperial Order of the Legion of Honor.

"You're one of the lucky ones, Father!" cried Father Toccanier happily. "Oh, how splendid!"

I did not agree, and when the cross and ribbon of the Legion of Honor arrived, I gave them to Father Tocanier. Nor would I wear them on Sundays and feast days as he begged me to do. Somehow I felt that God would be better pleased if I did without worldly honors and waited for the reward which He Himself had in store for me in Heaven.

"Besides, what have I done to merit this distinction from the Emperor?" I asked. "I, a poor parish priest, who hardly ever leaves his little village?"

"You've brought back thousands of sinners to God," declared Father Toccanier quickly. "Why, there's not a priest in France who has had your success in the confessional, Father. Not one."

I smiled at the childlike eagerness. My assistant was a fine young man, yet at times he seemed to forget that any success I had had in Ars was due solely to God's grace, not to any merits of mine. Then an unexpected thought struck me.

"I was ordained when I was twenty-nine years old," I said slowly, "but there was one sacred function which I was not allowed to perform during the first months of my priesthood. Of course you've heard what it was?"

There was silence as Father Toccanier shifted awkwardly. "You . . .you weren't allowed to hear Confessions, Father?"

"That's right, my son. And why not?"

"Well . . ."

"Come, now. Speak out plainly."

"The authorities didn't think that you were experienced enough, Father."

"Ah, you mean they knew that I couldn't pass the necessary examinations."

"Oh, no, Father! That wasn't it at all."

I patted the arm of my young curate. "I think it was. And as far as that goes, it was only because of the extreme shortage of priests that the Vicar General ever let me be ordained. You see, I was dreadfully slow at books. And after all these years I'm still very poor at Latin. The Emperor—well, I guess he doesn't know all this."

Father Toccanier listened respectfully, but it was only too clear that he was not putting much stock in what I said. He had a deep and sincere affection for me, like that of a loyal son for his father, and he really believed that I deserved the honor which the Emperor had given me. It was a great disappointment to him that I would not wear such a distinguished decoration.

As the weeks of 1855 passed by, it seemed as though I had not an enemy in the whole world. Only friends were mine—hundreds of friends, thousands of friends! Each mail brought requests from them for prayers and Masses. Then one day a new friend came to see me. He was Brother Joseph Babey, a Marianist. His superiors had sent him to Ars to ask my prayers for Joseph Vaucher, a sick pupil.

It was easy to see that Brother Babey was much concerned over his young charge. However, in just a short time I was able to set his mind at ease. And why? Because as was so often the case, God had allowed me to have a glimpse into the future. Thus I suddenly knew for a certainty that young Joseph Vaucher (now at death's door from typhoid fever) would recover. In fact, in a few months he himself would come to Ars to thank Saint Philomena for the restoration of his health.

At my words Brother Babey was almost overcome. What splendid news to send back to his superiors! To the whole grieving Vaucher family! But there was also something else. . .

"Write or telegraph the boy's mother about his recovery, and then come back and we'll talk about your own troubles," I said encouragingly.

The young religious obeyed, and that night came to me a second time. But despite his relief over the case of Joseph Vaucher, he was still far from being happy. So many things were worrying him! For instance, his superiors were urging that he study for the priesthood, although he himself felt a dreadful fear of the responsibilities involved, particularly those of the confessional. Then again, he sometimes felt that perhaps he should leave the Marianists and become a missionary or a catechist in some foreign country. After all, the Society of Mary was a comparatively new religious organization and as yet had not been finally approved by the Church.

My heart went out to the worried young man before me. "You're a Brother of Mary—a Marianist!" I exclaimed. "Oh, my son! What a beautiful vocation! What a beautiful Society!"

Brother Babey's eyes widened. "You know it, then?"

"Of course I know it. This Society, among others, is called to do a great deal of good in the Church. It will exist until the end of the world, and all the religious who die in it will go to Heaven."

"But Father, my superiors want me to be a priest, and somehow I feel that I haven't the necessary health."

I put my hand on Brother Babey's shoulder. "You've heard about Saint Philomena?"

"Oh, yes, Father."

"You have a great devotion to her?"

"Well . . ."

"My son, you will recite the *Veni Creator*, the *Memorare* and an Our Father for nine days in her honor, and leave the matter of your health in God's hands. You are going to be a priest in the Society of Mary. Take care never to leave it."

For a moment Brother Babey stared at me in amazement. Then slowly, joyful tears welled up in his eyes. The new little religious family to which he belonged—the Marianists—was destined for great things! It would exist until the end of the world and all the religious who would die in it would go to Heaven! Even more. Despite all the recent doubts and temptations, he himself had been given the great gift of a priestly vocation. All that was necessary was to remain obedient to his superiors and to cooperate with the many new graces which presently would come his way.

"Father, how can I thank you for what you've told me?" he burst out suddenly. "Why. . .why, I feel like a new person!"

I smiled. "Just ask the Blessed Mother—the patroness of your beautiful Society—to help me to do my work well," I said.

Brother Babey agreed, then looked at me strangely. "But surely there is something else that I can do for you, Father! A small gift, perhaps? A service of some kind?"

I shook my head firmly. "No, my son, just say a Hail Mary for me once in a while. Oh, if you only knew the power for good that lies in that little prayer—especially when it is said with real love!"

Of course Brother Babey was not the only one in whom I urged a devotion to the Blessed Mother. All my life I had done my best to foster a great love for her in the hearts of those who came to me. Now as I grew older and realized that my time on earth was drawing to a close, I redoubled my efforts. In fact, hardly a day went by that I did not mention Our Lady's name, either in the pulpit or in the confessional. Yet, despite all my work in the Blessed Mother's cause, I continued to meet people who professed that they did not love her—and who certainly never gave her a thought from one day to the next.

"What a dreadful pity!" I told one of these poor souls, a young woman who came to me one autumn day in the year 1858. "My child, don't you know that Our Lady loves you more than any creature in the whole world loves you? That she is kinder and more eager to help you to be happy than your best friend?"

The newcomer looked at me respectfully, then sighed and shook her head. "It may be as you say, Father, but somehow I just can't feel any devotion to the Blessed Virgin. She seems too far away. She...she's too *cold!*"

"My poor child, you are the one who is cold," I said. "Tell me—do you ever say the Rosary?"

"Sometimes, Father, but without much interest. And with many distractions."

I was silent for a moment. Then, as I had done thousands of times before, I suggested that my young friend make a novena to the Heart of Mary—the Immaculate Heart which, of all human hearts, has ever been a worthy temple of the Holy Ghost, the Spirit of Love.

"Ask Our Lady to warm your coldness with that perfect love of God that burns within her," I said. "After all, she is the most wonderful mother who ever lived. Her heart is so tender that those of all other mothers are but a morsel of ice in comparison."

Later in the day I felt impelled to speak publicly on the Blessed Virgin, for surely there were also other souls in the congregation who did not know or love her?

"Oh, my friends, devotion to Our Lady softens the heart!" I cried. "It is sweet! It is stimulating!"

Then again: "When our hands have touched perfume, they perfume everything with which they come in contact. If we pass our prayers through the hands of the Blessed Virgin, they will assume a fragrance they lack at present."

Finally: "One would not enter a house without a word to the doorkeeper. Well, the Blessed Virgin is the doorkeeper to Heaven. She is all mercy and love. She only desires to see us happy. All we have to do to be heard is to turn to her. . ."

Through God's grace my little talk touched many hearts. Then some weeks later the young woman who had insisted that she had never had any devotion to the Blessed Mother sought me out a second time. But now her whole being radiated a peace and joy that were wonderful to behold.

"Father, for the first time in my life I feel that I have a friend who will never fail me," she declared earnestly. "For the first time in my life I feel really secure."

My heart sang at these happy words. "Child, tell me all about it," I urged. "Tell me everything!"

There was not much to tell. For nine days, as I had suggested, my young friend had offered a decade of the Rosary in honor of the Immaculate Heart of Mary. She had recited the Hail Marys as carefully

"NOW I UNDERSTAND ABOUT
THE BLESSED MOTHER."

and as fervently as possible, without experiencing anything unusual. She had also made a second novena, and a third, still without feeling any particular attraction for the Blessed Mother. Then suddenly everything had changed.

"It was just as though something melted inside me, Father," she confessed. "In a flash I understood about the Blessed Mother."

"You understood what about her?"

"That she is kind! That she loves us! And that she never punishes us, no matter how dreadful our sins, but only pleads with her Son for forgiveness!"

"Ah, so you no longer think that the Blessed Mother is far away from you? That she is...well, *cold?*"

"Oh, no, Father! She is near! And the best and truest of friends!"

"And what caused this...this change?"

"I think that it was saying the Hail Mary, Father—as carefully and as fervently as I could. Oh, what a wonderful little prayer it is!"

Naturally my heart rejoiced over the "conversion" of my young friend, and I continued to advise all those who came to me to have a great faith in the Blessed Mother and to increase this faith by praying the Hail Mary frequently and fervently. But even as I did so, a certain anxiety filled my heart. Surely my days on earth for working for souls were just about over?

"I'm seventy-three years old," I told myself one night when I was worn out after more than eighteen hours of hearing Confessions. "Dearest Mother, I don't think I can do much more...even for you..."

CHAPTER TWENTY

The End of the Road

S UMMER came to Ars, the summer of 1859.
I grew constantly weaker. Now I could hardly
drag myself from the rectory to the church and
back again. There were times when I all but fainted
away in the midst of hearing Confessions. But God
gave me the strength to persevere, so that never was
it necessary for me to send away anyone who needed
help. On those days when the heat was so oppressive
that I felt I could not remain a moment longer in the
confessional, there were certain words which brought
me instant relief. I had learned them long ago as an
assistant to Father Balley in Ecully, and through the
years I had repeated them thousands of times:

*"If a priest should die as a result of his labors
and sufferings for God's glory and the salvation of
souls, it would not be a bad thing."*

On July 30, toward one o'clock in the morning,

I felt my strength ebbing as never before, and a strange certainty came to me that I should not offer the Holy Sacrifice again. My time on earth was just about over.

"I'm dying," I thought. *"Dying!"*

I reached out and rapped on the wall. Was I to go into eternity without having received the Last Rites to strengthen and console me on my way?

"Dear Lord, please don't let me leave this world without the Sacrament of Extreme Unction!" I begged. "Let someone hear my knocking so that a priest can be sent for. . .in time. . ."

Suddenly the door opened quietly and Catherine Lassagne peered in. Unknown to me, she had been keeping watch in the next room while Father Toccanier took a brief rest. At the sight of me, pale and scarcely able to breathe, she rushed forward.

"Father! What is it? What's wrong?"

"It's. . .it's my poor end," I whispered.

"Oh, no, Father!"

"Yes. Send someone for my confessor."

"But the doctor. . ."

"Don't bother him. He can do nothing."

Catherine would not listen, however, and before long an anxious little group was gathered about my bed: Doctor Saunier, who had attended me in my illness of sixteen years ago; Father Beau, who was parish priest at Jassans and who had acted as my confessor for more than thirteen years; Brothers Athanasius and Jerome, teachers in the local school for boys; and of course Father Toccanier, my loyal assistant.

"Saint Philomena will cure you, Father, just as she did before," the latter told me comfortingly.

"We'll have a novena of Masses," Brother Athanasius hastened to add, "special services in the church..."

Brother Jerome nodded vigorously. "Yes. Oh, Father! You must get better! You *must!*"

I made a feeble gesture. "No, no. It is impossible this time."

By mid-morning, all Ars knew about Doctor Saunier's report. If it were not so hot, I might be able to last a week or so. But since my heart was very weak and since the scorching weather which had been with us all through July showed no signs of abating...

"Two days, perhaps three," said the doctor. "Father Vianney can't last any longer than that."

My friends were heartbroken. In an effort to make my room more comfortable, a number of men climbed to the rectory roof and stretched heavy sheets of canvas from one side to the other. Hour after hour they kept soaking these with water, heedless of the blazing sunlight which beat down upon them.

"Poor souls!" I murmured. "Please tell them not to bother."

But the men would not leave their task. Nor would their wives and children cease to pray for my recovery. As for the pilgrims, many of them had come long distances to make their Confessions, to ask for advice, to beg me to intercede for them with Saint Philomena. Surely I was not going to disappoint them now by dying!

THEY KEPT SOAKING THE CANVAS WITH WATER.

"Father, do you suppose you could manage to bless the people from your bed?" asked Father Toccanier. "It would mean so much."

I nodded feebly, while a wave of joy filled my heart. How good still to be able to do something for souls!

So presently a bell was rung, and the crowds massed outside the rectory in the stifling heat fell upon their knees. Then, with my devoted assistant supporting my arm, I traced the Sign of the Cross and asked God to pour down His choicest gifts upon those who had come to Ars to see me. . .upon those who lived here. . .upon all who had ever visited our little church. . .or who would do so in the future. . .

"Let us all meet in Heaven," I begged silently.

The hours passed. Father Beau had heard my Confession shortly after his arrival in Ars on the morning of July 30. But despite Doctor Saunier's report that I had only a short while to live, he had hesitated to give me the Last Rites. Saint Philomena was going to cure me once more, he said. See what prayers were being offered for me in the church, in the streets, in every house in Ars! In a little while there would be a miracle. Strength would flow into my tired limbs. My heart would start to beat with renewed vigor. Despite my seventy-three years, I would rise up strong and well from my sickbed.

Yet on the afternoon of August 2, Father Beau gave in to my pleading. My pulse was now very weak. It was doubtful if I could live more than a few hours. Accompanied by some twenty priests, each with a lighted candle in his hand, he went down to the church to bring the Blessed Sacrament and the holy oil for Extreme Unction.

"How kind the good God is!" I murmured. "When we are no longer able to go to Him, He Himself comes to us."

Presently the church bell began to toll—a signal to the entire countryside that I was about to receive the Last Rites. At the somber sound, some of my friends watching in the room burst into tears. Saint Philomena hadn't worked a miracle after all! Now I was going to be taken from them! My body would be lowered into the dark ground! Never again would they be able to talk with me as friend to friend!

How my heart went out to these good souls! Oh, to have the strength to tell them my true feelings! All my life I, too, had been afraid of death, had dreaded appearing before the Judgment Seat of God, above all had trembled at the thought of falling into despair at the last moment. But now that my end was in sight there was no fear in me at all—only a deep joy and calm. However, since I could not speak except with extreme difficulty, I remained silent—reflecting upon words which I had used in the pulpit many times but which only now appeared to me in all their glorious truth:

"How sweet it is to die if one has lived on the cross!"

For several minutes the bell in the church tower continued to send its mournful tones through the oppressive stillness of the August afternoon. Then suddenly another sound caught my ear. It was a tiny, silvery tinkle—coming closer and closer—the signal that Father Beau was approaching with the Blessed Sacrament.

Before anyone could assist me, I had raised myself to a sitting position. Tears started from my eyes, as with folded hands I awaited the arrival of the little procession.

"My God!" I thought. *"My God!"*

Brother Elias, who was kneeling beside my bed, misunderstood the tears and tried to comfort me. "Father, why do you weep?" he asked gently. "In just a little while you'll be in Heaven."

The tinkling of the small bell grew louder, and the murmur of praying voices. "Yes, but it is sad to receive Holy Communion for the last time," I whispered.

However, in a few minutes I was myself again— filled with peace and joy. And though the heat in my little room was so intense that the twenty priests accompanying Father Beau were forced to put out their candles, I scarcely noticed the discomfort. Once again the Father, Son and Holy Ghost were with me in the most intimate manner possible in this life. Once again I was a Tabernacle of the Most High.

"This is the ending of all the roads in the world," I thought. *"And the beginning..."*

The hours passed. I received Extreme Unction, and the peace and joy within me grew. Those watching about my bed marveled that I still managed to cling to life; in fact, that I showed no signs of suffering or distress of any kind. Why, I did not even seem to notice the stifling heat, or the ominous rolls of thunder which shook the world from time to time as heavy clouds began to gather over Ars!

"Father Vianney's failing just the same," warned

the doctor. "He'll have gone from us by nightfall."

But the next day, August 3, I was able to prove my good friend wrong. In the afternoon when a lawyer and four witnesses came to inquire gently of me where I wished to be buried, I was able to understand and to give them an answer. "In Ars," I whispered. Then when the Bishop of Belley arrived around seven o'clock in the evening, I recognized him and by signs managed to ask for his blessing. But by ten o'clock it was thought best to begin the prayers for the dying. I united myself with these as well as I could, and at midnight kissed the crucifix which one of my friends held to my lips.

Two hours later, on August 4, the Feast of Saint Dominic, the storm which had been threatening Ars for so long broke in all its intensity. Jagged streaks of lightning cut through the black sky. The earth shook as thunder crashed on all sides. Sheets of rain lashed at the windows, and a wind of hurricane strength roared through the village streets. Yet within my little room all was peace as the prayers for the dying were recited for still another time.

> "May the heavens be opened to him, may the angels rejoice with him. Receive Thy servant, O Lord, into Thy kingdom. Let Saint Michael, the Archangel of God, who is the chief of the heavenly host, conduct him. Let the holy angels of God come forth to meet him, and bring him into the holy city of Jerusalem. . ."

I sighed and smiled. How good to be dying as

a priest! Forty-four years ago the Bishop had arranged the stole, the sign of the priestly office, about my neck and across my breast during the ceremony of Ordination.

"Take thou the yoke of the Lord, for His yoke is sweet and His burden light," he had said.

What wonderful words! The responsibilities of the priesthood were great, and the sacrifices required. But oh, the reward—the blessed reward—for helping others to know and to love the Heavenly Father! Only now was I beginning to understand.

St. Meinrad, Indiana
Feast of St. Meinrad
January 21, 1947

By the same author...

6 GREAT CATHOLIC BOOKS FOR CHILDREN

...and for all young people ages 10 to 100!!

1137 THE CHILDREN OF FATIMA—And Our Lady's Message to the World. 162 pp. PB. 15 Illus. Impr. The wonderful story of Our Lady's appearances to little Jacinta, Francisco and Lucia.   **6.00**

1138 THE CURÉ OF ARS—The Story of St. John Vianney, Patron Saint of Parish Priests. 211 pp. PB. 38 Illus. Impr. The many adventures that met young St. John Vianney when he set out to become a priest.   **9.00**

1139 THE LITTLE FLOWER—The Story of St. Therese of the Child Jesus. 167 pp. PB. 24 Illus. Impr. Tells what happened when little Therese decided to become a saint.   **7.00**

1140 PATRON SAINT OF FIRST COMMUNICANTS—The Story of Blessed Imelda Lambertini. 85 pp. PB. 14 Illus. Impr. Tells of the wonderful miracle God worked to answer little Imelda's prayer.   **4.00**

1141 THE MIRACULOUS MEDAL—The Story of Our Lady's Appearances to St. Catherine Labouré. 107 pp. PB. 21 Illus. Impr. The beautiful story of what happened when young Sister Catherine saw Our Lady.   **5.00**

1142 ST. LOUIS DE MONTFORT—The Story of Our Lady's Slave. 211 pp. PB. 20 Illus. Impr. The remarkable story of the priest who went around helping people become "slaves" to Jesus through Mary.   **9.00**

1143 THE SET (Reg. 40.00)   **32.00**

(Add $2.00 post./hdlg. for each order going to one address.)
Prices guaranteed through December 31, 1994.

TAN BOOKS AND PUBLISHERS, INC.
P. O. Box 424
Rockford, Illinois 61105
CALL TOLL FREE: 1-800-437-5876

MARY FABYAN WINDEATT

Mary Fabyan Windeatt could well be called the "storyteller of the saints," for such indeed she was. And she had a singular talent for bringing out doctrinal truths in her stories, so that without even realizing it, young readers would see the Catholic catechism come to life in the lives of the saints.

Mary Fabyan Windeatt wrote at least 21 books for children, plus the text of about 28 Catholic story coloring books. At one time there were over 175,000 copies of her books on the saints in circulation. She contributed a regular "Children's Page" to the monthly Dominican magazine, *The Torch*.

Miss Windeatt began her career of writing for the Catholic press around age 24. After graduating from San Diego State College in 1934, she had gone to New York looking for work in advertising. Not finding any, she sent a story to a Catholic magazine. It was accepted—and she continued to write. Eventually Miss Windeatt wrote for 33 magazines, contributing verse, articles, book reviews and short stories.

Having been born in 1910 in Regina, Saskatchewan, Canada, Mary Fabyan Windeatt received the Licentiate of Music degree from Mount Saint Vincent College in Halifax, Nova Scotia at age 17. With her family she moved to San Diego in that same year, 1927. In 1940 Miss Windeatt received an A.M. degree from Columbia University. Later, she lived with her mother near St. Meinrad's Abbey, St. Meinrad, Indiana. Mary Fabyan Windeatt died on November 20, 1979.

(Much of the above information is from Catholic Authors: Contemporary Biographical Sketches 1930-1947, *ed. by Matthew Hoehn, O.S.B., B.L.S., St. Mary's Abbey, Newark, N.J., 1957.)*